FALLING IN *Love*

How To Be In Love Without Falling

Vanessa Dale Coleman

First printing, September 2020

Published by Songs For Life Ministries (Book Division), St. Louis, Missouri
"Ministering for the life of you and yours" (Deuteronomy 30:19)
Working for the glory of God (Psalm 86:12) and edification of people (Ephesians 4:12)

© 2020, Vanessa Dale Coleman
Cover Design by Songs For Life Ministries (Graphic Division)

ISBN 978-0-9747641-1-5
Printed in United States of America

Unless otherwise indicated, all scripture quotations are taken from *The Holy Bible: King James Version*

Scripture quotations marked (AMP) are taken from the *Amplified Bible,* Copyright © 1954, 1958, 1962, 1964, 1965, 1987 by The Lockman Foundation. Used by permission.

Scripture quotations marked (NIV) are taken from the Holy Bible, *New International Version*®, NIV®. Copyright © 1973, 1978, 1984, 2011 by Biblica, Inc.® Used by permission of Zondervan.

Scripture quotations marked (NKJV) are taken from The Holy Bible, New King James Version®. Copyright © 1982 by Thomas Nelson. Used by permission. All rights reserved.

Greek & Hebrew Definitions taken from *Zodhiates' Hebrew Greek Key Study Bible Lexical Aids to the Old Testament*

All rights reserved. No part of this book may be reproduced or transmitted in any form or by any means without written permission from the author.

DEDICATION

This book is dedicated to the many people, of all ages, who continue to participate in the seemingly endless search for love and the proverbial *"happy-ever-after"* romantic relationship. I pray that your eyes will be opened to an enlightened view. This view will cause you to avoid unnecessarily hurtful, time-consuming falls of various degrees. It will cause an increase of healthy, thriving, fruitful love relationships that are built on the Word of God and His way of loving for generations to come.

"And [I pray] that the eyes of your heart [the very center and core of your being] may be enlightened [flooded with light by the Holy Spirit], so that you will know and cherish the hope [the divine guarantee, the confident expectation] to which He has called you, the riches of His glorious inheritance in the saints (God's people),..."
(Ephesians 1:18 AMP)

TABLE OF CONTENTS

Dedication	iii
Special Thanks	vii
Pre-Publication Reviews	viii
Introduction	xiv
Chapter 1 What's Love Got To Do With It	1
Chapter 2 Emotional Malnutrition/Suicide Struggles	7
Chapter 3 Sexual Activity - Today	17
Chapter 4 Sexual Activity - Yesterday	21
Chapter 5 Types of Love - Know the Difference	31
Chapter 6 The Goal – "Happily Ever After"	43
Chapter 7 The Close Call	53
Chapter 8 The Marriage Blessing	59
Chapter 9 Grow In Love With God	65
Chapter 10 Establish Your Lifeline	73
Chapter 11 Growth and Development	79
Chapter 12 Be In Love With You	91
Chapter 13 You Are Always Enough	97
Chapter 14 Illegitimate But Ordained	103
Chapter 15 Learn To Love All People	109
Chapter 16 Learn To Forgive All People	115
About the Author	121
Suggested Reading	122
Songs For Life Products	123

SPECIAL THANKS

To Chester Coleman, my awesome husband, who has shown me time and time and time again what it means to love and be loved without condition. You have consistently lived out Ephesians 5:25 throughout our entire marriage. Your support, sacrifice and willingness to allow me to do whatever, whenever required, is amazing! I love you to life and will continue until the second coming of our Lord, Jesus Christ or until death do us part!

"Husbands, love your wives [seek the highest good for her and surround her with a caring, unselfish love], just as Christ also loved the Church and gave Himself up for her,..."
(Ephesians 5:25 AMP)

To my Pastor, Pricellious J. Burruss and the late Dr. Richard Burruss. God has used both mightily from the day I was born again and throughout these years. You have taught and fed me with knowledge and understanding of His Word and how I ought to daily live in Christ Jesus. I am eternally grateful for your spiritual leadership, Godly example, and the many, many deposits that brought me out of lack and into abundant life.

"And I will set up shepherds over them which shall feed them: and they shall fear no more, nor be dismayed, neither shall they be lacking, saith the Lord." (Jeremiah 23:4 NKJV)

To all who took time from your busy schedules to preview, proof and probe this work. Your input has been of great value in manifesting a desire to produce a life-changing tool to help people to obtain and maintain *REAL LOVE* without *FALLING!* Know that any life-changing fruit that results goes to your account as well.

PRE-PUBLICATION REVIEWS

This book feeds the spirit, stimulates the mind, stabilizes the emotions and brings self-control to the flesh. The various angles and plethora of information Minister Vanessa presents, points to the need and benefits of knowing "*HOW TO BE IN LOVE WITHOUT FALLING.*"

I was born again by the Spirit of God and surrendered my life to Jesus at 19 years old. I have been married and now widowed. The majority of my adult life I have lived as an unmarried Christian. By the grace of God by living out 1 Thessalonians 4:1-5 as an unmarried believer, I have not fallen into sexual sin and was spared from the consequences noted in this life-changing book. It will be a game changer for you if you apply the principles to your everyday life!
Pastor Pricellious J. Burruss
Transformation Christian Church & World Outreach Center

"*Falling In Love - How To Be In Love Without Falling*" – Can you relate to how you know you will watch a movie in it's entirety just from the previews? Well, I know I will read this book just from what I previewed. It is difficult to express or explain truth without transparency. Thank you for sharing your struggles all the way to your victory as it pertains to real love.

Love is not a second-hand emotion but is essential to living. It is the ultimate feel-good drug that we all desire. That was one of my favorite takeaways. The road we travel in pursuit of love can be a journey to be reckoned with, full of rejection, depression, and even suicidal thoughts and actions, as you point out in your book. Lost lives and love that could be known is a sad commentary. Your book is illustrated proof that this can be avoided. I lost my young nephew this way. He just could not figure out true love when it came to opposite gender relationships and took his own life.

Your book will benefit so many. We underestimate the power of rejection as it pertains to spiritual and mental issues. Thanks for showing us that these difficult issues can be conquered!

Men will read this book because we experience everything that you expressed through your transparency, but it is covered up under the armor of what we call being a man. Anything that falls can break! Thanks for revealing to us that we *can* love without falling.
<u>Bishop Herman Tolar</u>
Disciple Fellowship Christian Church

Let me first start out by saying, this book is amazingly captivating from the start. I love how the two main words in the phrase *"falling in love"* are broken down and detailing their contradictory meanings. Coming from someone who loves learning and knowledge that alone was very much appreciated. As an unmarried young woman, there's a lot more for me to learn about love than I thought. This book is going to be life changing to a lot of receptive hearts.
<u>Ms. Laquita Allen</u>
St. Louis, Missouri

This book is a *MUST READ*! In addition to true revelation about love, it contains real life experiences that take you on a journey as to why there are so many failed marriages. It gives true biblical truths and principles that will help any sincere couple to have a loving and blessed marriage.
<u>Pastor Gerry Anderson</u>
Kingdom Life Ministries

"Falling In Love – How to Be In Love Without Falling" is a must read for those who want to experience real love without all the

Falling In Love – How To Be In Love Without Falling

pitfalls that accompany engaging in wrong relationships. As we navigate through a world that is constantly attempting to redefine love, it is paramount that we remain constant in our convictions of how God defines and displays love. We must emulate His behavior in all of our love relationships. This masterful work challenges the reader to reconsider the process of falling in love by reminding us that rarely does anything positive accompany a fall. Minister Vanessa eloquently describes the benefits of real love without the fall as she parallels the process of her love for God, herself, and her husband.

This book will be helpful for singles, married couples, those battling depression, loneliness and low self-worth. Minister Vanessa's transparent account of her *"fall"* serves as a cautionary tale to others to love on God's terms. She encourages couples to grow into love rather than falling. She describes being in love verses falling in love, differentiates lust from love and defines the various types of love.

This is a great tool to help you understand love and those who say they love you. It inspires you to seek and cultivate a love relationship with God, the very definition of love. 21 years after my Christian conversion, this book motivated me to develop a deeper love for God, others and myself.

<u>Minister Cortaiga S. Collins</u>
Author of "To All My Baby Mamas"
Owner of Good Shepherd Preschool & Infant/Toddler Center

I believe that this book is relevant, without regard to age or gender. It can alleviate a lot of heartache and bring wholeness if it is indeed adhered to by the reader. It is a great, biblically based, conversation starter. If you're looking for love, read this book.

<u>Minister Dale Spiva</u>
Transformation Christian Church & World Outreach Center

<u>Falling In Love – How To Be In Love Without Falling</u>

I started reading your manuscript and couldn't stop. I was so encouraged with your revelation of the true meaning of *"falling in love."* I never saw it in this vein before! I hope your book becomes a bestseller. The information is life-changing and you centered the information of love according to GOD and his WORD.

<u>Pastor Melody Anderson</u>
Kingdom Life Ministries

"Becoming Whole" are the first words that come to my mind as I read, *"Falling in Love - How To Be In Love Without Falling."* In this book, Vanessa provides spiritual and practical guidance on how to seek, receive, and walk in deliverance from the expectations and disappointments of love that may have been experienced. She explains how various weapons are *"formed"* to keep people entrapped in a cycle of distorted love until the realization that the cycle must be broken.

We learn through the revelations herein that Satan uses his weapons on us as early as possible in life. Thanks be to God; through Jesus and His blood, those who have accepted Him as Savior have overcome Satan!

This is a beautiful book. As you read, you will experience a series of emotions and thoughts. In the end, praise is given to God for the work He has done in Minister Vanessa and will do in you. I recommend it to women, men, Christians and non-Christians alike.

Lastly, I highly recommend it to parents to learn from Vanessa's experiences and to seek God in prayer and through seeking Godly wisdom about how to talk to their children about sex and intimacy. Also, to pray that their children seek God to obtain a revelation from Him about real love, sexuality, sex, and intimacy. I know as you read "Falling in Love - How To Be In Love Without Falling," you will be blessed. Enjoy!   *<u>Mrs. Rose Horn</u>*
Denver, Colorado

Falling In Love – How To Be In Love Without Falling

What a wonderful book. We love how Vanessa Coleman weaves the stories of her own love experiences with meaningful scriptures that open and reveal God's heart. This is simply a must-read for every woman and man, especially if you have fallen prone to society's image and suggestions about love and romance. It's time to stop falling in love, and learn how to GROW in love -- God's way. Herein is help to do just that!

Pastor/Author Alfred T. Long
Pastor/Author/Radio Host Kacie Starr Long
Inspired Overflow Ministries

In her usual straightforward, profound style, Minister Vanessa Dale Coleman has "hit the ball out of the park" on this book! I love how she weaves parts of her life and pertinent Scriptures throughout the entire book. In addition, she is not afraid to bare her own soul in the hopes of turning many to truth and righteousness. Vanessa leaves no stone unturned concerning this *"hot"* topic and addresses it in a complete fashion. This is a book you will not be able to put down, and one that you will long remember even after you have put it down—because her words and wisdom speak directly to the heart! This book is a much-needed resource for pastors, and especially recommended for those who pastor older youth and college-age young people.

Reverends/Authors Patricia & Vito Rallo
Free Indeed Ministries

Our friend, Minister Vanessa Dale Coleman, anointed Worship leader, Psalmist and now for the second time, Author, has beautifully combined biblical teaching on marriage, sex and love to give us a better understanding of true love so as not to *"fall"* into a detrimental trap that pulls us out of the will of God.

Minister Vanessa has created a wealth of information including personal experiences for those desiring the perfect will of God in

Falling In Love – How To Be In Love Without Falling

romantic relationships. God is grooming or has groomed the "perfect fit" for you. Not the perfect person because those folks don't exist! God knows who is right for you. He knows what you like too! *(Gen. 2:22)*. Don't let the mainstream media teach you and your children about love, sex, and marriage.

You can save your marriage before it starts by reading and applying the principles outlined in this book!

Pastors David and Pamela Ruck
The Glory Church

Vanessa Dale Coleman shines a biblical light on how words have been used in repetition, either through conversations, or lyrically in music, that contradict the Word of God. This hinders the ability for the born-again believer to move forward in their journey in Christ Jesus.

She boldly enlightens and reminds the reader by defining and clearly explaining the meaning of the words *"fall"* and *"falling."* It paints clarity that life and death are truly in the power of the tongue. **Herein she** challenges and compels the reader with biblical relevance that words and what we speak shape our world in every area, specifically our relationships.

She transparently connects with those who have struggled or may be struggling with rejection, suicidal thoughts, and emotional issues by sharing her personal testimony. Here it is proven that ONLY through a personal relationship with our Lord and Savior Jesus Christ, can one be truly free from the grips of the emotional pain and hurt of their past. *Minister Howard Hernandez Woodard*
Transformation Christian Church & World Outreach Center

INTRODUCTION

"Falling in love" is an age-old term that describes the process that people go through while developing a relationship that is headed for romantic, mental, emotional, and physical intimacy. Most people tend to use this phrase when they become infatuated or begin to feel a strong emotional attraction or bond to another person, generally of the opposite gender. The process seems to have high priority in the minds of many who aspire to encounter the proverbial 'true love' or 'soul mate' to share in your life. It's one of those universal statements that warrant little attention to what is actually being stated.

Let's take the time to break down the phrase, *"falling in love"* through a word study.

Looking closely at the word *"fall,"* we find there is very little, if any, good in it. Merriam-Webster's definition of *"fall"* is as follows:

> *"To drop or descend under...as to a lower place through loss or lack of support; to drop down suddenly to a lower position; to leave a standing or erect position suddenly, whether voluntarily or not; become of a lower level, degree, amount, value; extend downward, to be directed downward; to succumb to temptation or sin becoming unchaste or to lose one's innocence; to lose status, dignity, position, character, etc.; to be overthrown; to drop down wounded or dead; to pass into some failing physical, mental, or emotional condition."*

Primarily, the word *"fall"* speaks of decrease, failure and pain. In any connotation it says, *"You're going down fast."* It doesn't

Falling In Love – How To Be In Love Without Falling

matter if you're speaking of a person, place, or thing. Every example of the word in any dictionary speaks of decline, failure, disappointment, sorrow, loss, and discord and like terms. *"To fall,"* says that you're off balance and can't stand your ground.

The word "love," is opposite in meaning of the word "fall." Love speaks of everything that is good, perfect and uplifting. It edifies, builds up, and adds worth and value. Using the two words, love and fall, in the same sentence is contradictory. However, because of the seeming appropriateness and overwhelming popularity of the statement "falling in love," it is spoken over and over and over again when referring to romantic relationships.

"Death and life are in the power of the tongue, and those who love it will eat its fruit."
(Proverbs 18:21 NKJV)

"...Words are powerful; take them seriously. Words can be your salvation. Words can also be your damnation."
(Matthew 12:37 MSG)

Could it be that speaking the phrase *"falling in love"* subconsciously assists, or sets into motion, a process of demise to the relationship at hand?

Let's take a look at the following statement written by Kevin J. Harris in his blog titled, "Fresh Thinking:"

> *From 100 couples on a first date, in 3 months time 85% of these couples will no longer be together or talking to each other. At this point there are only 15 of 100 couples remaining.*
>
> *At the 6 month marker about 50% will be broken up. This leaves 8 couples.*
>
> *4 couples will make it to 1 year. That is 4% of the original group.*
>
> *2 of the 4 couples will wind up getting married or in a common law situation.*
>
> *After 5 years only 1 couple is still together.*

Falling In Love – How To Be In Love Without Falling

Considering these statistics, the statement *"falling in love"* could be a factor of detriment that has not been considered by most.

Wikipedia has an interesting excerpt concerning the *"falling in love"* term:

> *"In romantic relationships, falling in love is mainly a Western concept of moving from a feeling of neutrality towards a person to one of love. The use of the term "fall" implies that the process is in some way inevitable, uncontrollable, risky, irreversible, and that it puts the lover in a state of vulnerability, in the same way the word "fall" is used in the phrase "to fall ill" or "to fall into a trap." (en.wikepedia.wiki/Falling_in_Love)*

This definition makes me laugh a bit because it reminds me of all of the uncontrollable, risky, and failed so-called "love" relationships I was involved in prior to receiving Christ. In light of its contradictory nature, and in spite of its popularity, could it be a factor in the progressively worsening breakup and divorce rate in the world, as well as in the Body of Christ, the Church?

You may be thinking, "Who cares anyway? *'Falling in love'* is just a statement, a simple expression of emotions. Vanessa, you're going too far. Everybody wants to *'fall in love'* someday." Certainly, I had never given much, if any, thought to it until it came to my attention while preparing a Bible lesson to teach to a group of singles at my local church.

Yes, who does care? I venture to say whether you are a person who takes the words spoken over your life seriously, or not, you might reconsider and exact a bit of care about its use in your vocabulary. This would be especially true if you're desiring a *"happily ever after"* relationship as opposed to a heartbreaking *"fall."* Even if that's not your current desire, if you're human, you've got to have love. It's true whether you are the one searching or the one being searched for. No matter your ethnicity, age or gender, there is desire in various degrees. It follows the age-old process of attraction, infatuation and ultimate growth into real love that endures. Unfortunately, premature and inappropriate sex is often the primary thing that leads to a fall prior to experiencing real love.

"Falling in love" is a difficult subject to tackle in these times when so many people are desperate for love yet many are void of morality. Many are being deceived and deprived of the purity of true love as intended by God who is the essence and originator of it. Yes, we are in a time where superficial love is being displayed in many "trendy" ways. Nevertheless, the Holy Bible is *STILL* very clear on things like sexuality and marriage. If even one person can be influenced to change a flesh-driven, trendy view of a romantic relationship to a Godly one, it is well worth my time, effort and resources. If a mind and heart can be motivated and changed to allow God to, at the very least, be involved at the foundation of the relationship choices, this labor of love will have been successful.

My prayer for you is that you will be found, above all things, growing in your love relationship with God through Jesus Christ. Subsequently, you can be led into an eventual romantic love relationship that will build you up and enhance your life. It can be purposeful in many ways without causing you to *"fall."*

CHAPTER 1
WHAT'S LOVE GOT TO DO WITH IT?

To fall in love, what a delight,
To fall in love, searching all my life,
To fall in love is the ultimate flight,
To fall, to fall, to fall, in love!'
(V.D. Coleman)

What's love got to do with it anyway? According to Tina Turner, the pop singer, in her song titled "What's Love Got To Do With It" (written by Graham Lyle), love is a "second hand emotion" and a "sweet old fashioned, notion" that inevitably leads to a broken heart. Who wants to end up with a broken heart? No one! The world listened to it over and over again *(me included)*, danced to it, cried to it, loved and broke up to it.

Because of what I have learned and experienced with God and His word, I beg to differ with Mrs. Turner, who performs the song so convincingly. Truth is, love has everything to do with any mutually respectable relationship, particularly romantic ones with real substance and stamina.

The song is incorrect. Love is a real and powerful, *'first-hand emotion'* that carries, what I call, spiritual, mental and emotional side effects. This is expressed in the following excerpt from an Internet article titled, *"Love Without the Falling,"* by Acamea Deadwiler, a secular behavioral coach:

Falling In Love – How To Be In Love Without Falling

"Love is one of our most powerful and least understood emotions — especially in the romantic sense. It can hit us without warning. Love can co-exist with conflicting emotions, like anger, annoyance and sadness. Meaning we can be extremely upset with someone, they can hurt us, we can even want nothing more to do with them and yet, somehow, still love them. People exhibit over-the-top, out of character behavior, all in the name of love.

Love is real. So real that a biological anthropologist studied 166 societies and found evidence of formidable, blissful, romantic love in 147 of them. This indicates to many medical professionals that romantic love is an essential element of our biological nature.

Our bodies exhibit scientifically proven physical reactions to the feeling, such as flushed cheeks, a racing heartbeat and sweaty palms. There are also chemical responses happening within us that signify love (the emotion) may be in the air, including the release of Dopamine, Norepinephrine (otherwise known as adrenalin) and Serotonin — the chemical which when low can lead to depression. Research shows that love gives us a sense of happiness! And excitement. It is the ultimate feel-good drug.

Because of these reactions, we believe that whom we choose as a partner is at the mercy of our subconscious biochemistry. We can't tell our "love chemicals" not to produce or our hands not to get clammy. We can't keep those butterflies from somehow finding their way into our bellies. So, there is a consensus that the feeling of love is beyond our realm of influence."

Falling In Love – How To Be In Love Without Falling

Ms. Deadwiler has some valid points in her articles, which verify my *"side effect"* theory. Nonetheless if you allow your emotions and physical attractions to lead, you're definitely headed for a *"fall."* Emotions fluctuate consistently and can be misleading. They come and they go.

There was another song that was super popular titled, *"You're Nobody 'Til Somebody Loves You."* It was written by James Cavanaugh, Larry Stock, and Russ Morgan and made popular by Dean Martin. It was an extremely simple but highly publicized song. The gist of the song was in the title. It wasn't necessarily my cup of tea in music, but when I did hear it somehow, it stuck with me. When I really think about it, it was one of those subtle lies that many people bought into. Yes, it too was *just a song* but listening to it and singing it over and over again, would definitely deposit that lie into your subconscious and spirit.

> *You're nobody 'til somebody loves you,*
> *You're nobody 'til somebody cares,*
> *You're nobody 'til somebody loves you,*
> *So find yourself somebody to love.*

There's no need to find somebody to love you. That's part of the problem, looking for love in the wrong way and places and finding trouble! The truth is, somebody already loves you and cares deeply for you, so much so that He gave His life for you. His name is Jesus Christ.

> *"For God so loved the world that He gave His only begotten Son that whosoever believeth in Him should not perish but have everlasting life." (John 3:16)*

> *"For I am persuaded, that neither death, nor life, nor angels, nor principalities, nor powers, nor things present, nor things to come, nor height, nor depth, nor any other*

Falling In Love – How To Be In Love Without Falling

creature, shall be able to separate us from the love of God, which is in Christ Jesus our Lord."
(Romans 8:38-39 NKJV)

With all of the tradition out there about *"finding somebody"* and *"falling in love,"* would you agree that we all have a lot to learn about true love and its many-splendored nature? Thus, another song title comes to mind, "Love Is a Many Splendored Thing." It is indeed "splendored" in that it is powerful, magnificent, brilliant, engaging, life changing, transforming, and all consuming, to say the very least. Because of WHO LOVE IS *(GOD)*, He is all that and so much more! Just think about it, you were created by and for Love.

We should do our best to learn what Love has to say about all of its types. This is especially true of romantic love, since it seems to be the type that leads so many into repeated *"falls"* in life. It stands to reason that if you know what and who you're really looking for, you might locate a love that will endure in today's society. Although you want to *"be* in love" romantically at some point in your life, it is not something you want to *"fall"* into though you may stumble upon it.

"So God created man in His own image, in the image of God created He him; male and female created He them. And God blessed them, and God said unto them, be fruitful, and multiply, and replenish the earth,..."
(Genesis 1:27,28a)

"Let us love one another, for love comes from God. Everyone who loves has been born of God and knows God. Whoever does not love does not know God, because God is Love. . . . . And so we know and rely on the love

Falling In Love – How To Be In Love Without Falling

God has for us. God is love. Whoever lives in love lives in God, and God in them." (I John 4:7,8,16 NIV)

Infused into every member of the human race of any and every ethnicity, is the ability, desire and deep-seated need to love and be loved. From the womb to the tomb, you are divinely and quite naturally wired to receive love and to give love in one capacity or another. Because God is love and every person is created in His image, it is vital that you receive love and that you give love throughout your life. I would venture to say that, in a sense, it is much like the need for oxygen to breathe. You've got to have it or you will die. Although you won't physically die without human love, your life will definitely be missing an essential, life-enhancing element. Without it, you'll be emotionally malnourished. Malnourishment leads to death by starvation. Love is indeed a necessity for every person on the planet.

CHAPTER 2
EMOTIONAL MALNUTRITION AND SUICIDE STRUGGLES

Life without love is not living,
Life without love is so sad,
Life without love leaves you empty,
Life without love hurts so bad,
But there's someone who always loves you,
His Name is the essence of Love,
No need to take your life or live without,
Look to the Father of Lights from above!
(V.D. Coleman)

Though there are many, one of the motivations for suicidal thoughts is emotional malnutrition and the feeling of being unloved. Heavy demonic influence *(Ephesians 6:12)* contributes to feelings of hopelessness, lack of joy and purpose. Of course, there are some suicidal tendencies that stem from mental illnesses, possibly caused by chemical imbalance in the brain and other physical issues. There are few things more crushing than the emotional pain of feeling unloved and rejected by someone you believed you were in love with. Things like rejection and abandonment can lead to spiritual and mental issues that can destroy the desire to live and work through life's difficult issues.

One young lady, after reading a draft of this book, shared an interesting take on why she had once contemplated suicide. She said, *"Lack of love is not my issue by the way. I feel more disconnected from life itself as well as people in general. Many times I just don't see the point of my personal creation or existence."* This is yet another deceptive motivation that could produce suicidal tendencies. This simply boils down to lack of knowledge of one's purpose and love for self, even when feeling loved by others.

When I was 17 years old or so, I experienced my first of two suicide attempts. I cringe when I think about the thoughts and unsettling emotions that constantly plagued me during those times. Talk about *"falling!"*

After falling into the sin of fornication *(sex outside of marriage)* and becoming pregnant, I experienced much rejection from the boy I had been sexually intimate with for months. He was my first, and I truly thought he loved me, or at least I really wanted him to. Along with the pregnancy and rejection came so much shame it was unreal. No matter who was around me, my mind was inundated with thoughts of being unloved, not only by the boy who had impregnated me, but everyone else. This was due to my overwhelming shame. It was mentally and emotionally tormenting, painful, depressing and draining. At the core of every one of those tormenting thoughts and emotions was the thought, *"nobody loves me."* Of course this was a lie that seemed like absolute truth in my mind. Because the one person I thought I needed most to love me did not, it affected my view of all of my relationships, including the way I related to myself within myself. One of the deep-seated issues was that I didn't love myself. This made me very needy, emotionally unattractive and easily deceived. I entered this love relationship with the wrong perspective of myself and it automatically positioned me for a *fall*. I began to view myself as absolutely worthless and after a while it became true in my mind. It was indeed one of the lowest points of my life. I felt unloved, rejected, alone, stupid, worthless and totally misused throughout my pregnancy and beyond.

My first *"falling in love"* experience with someone who only lusted for me resulted in years of heartache. Not only was there heartache for me, but also for my son who was conceived, carried and born out of the dysfunction, rejection and pain of that *"fall."* That poor child also suffered rejection and neglect because of the dysfunction and foolishness I had fallen into.

When I think back, there was emptiness in my heart and life long before I met this so-called *"first love"* in the form of my son's father. The emptiness was one thing that made him so attractive and irresistible in the first place. I was much too immature and vulnerable to have even entered such a relationship.

In any case, after the pregnancy announcement, everything started deteriorating quickly. There was initially no support or acknowledgment of joy, happiness and acceptance. There was only avoidance, rejection, and more shame. My goodness, there was also so much fear as I had to push to be a part of not only his life, but also life in general. On top of all of the hormonal emotions that naturally come with pregnancy, which should be a happy time, I felt I had little if any reason to wake up each day. Not only was there struggle in the waking hours, I was troubled at night with horrible dreams mostly about my absentee boyfriend. The dreams consistently caused sleeplessness.

A very painful memory of the *falling* relationship comes to mind. I had to drop out of school and go into a special program for pregnant girls. I was walking home in the rain one day and tears were flowing down my face as I stopped at a phone booth to make yet another call that was unanswered. There I was, a fat, pregnant, abandoned, teenage girl standing all alone in the rain at a phone booth. There had been no phone calls or visits from him for weeks. He was never home whenever I called, no matter what time it was. There were rumors of other girls he was seeing and my so-called friends made sure I had reports of how much fun he was having without me. It was the ultimate time of rejection and feelings of abandonment.

One evening soon after my "rainy day" experience, I was having one of my many private pity parties when the phone rang. What I heard on the other end of the phone was a phrase from a song by Nancy Wilson, *"Face It Girl, It's over."* There was no conversation, just the song's title chorus being played, and then a click as the phone was hung up. Of course, it was my so-called boyfriend giving me the final boot without saying a word himself. Talk about a *fall*; or better described, a painful, humiliating *crash*. After calling back multiple times with no answer, I faced reality and cried myself to sleep. I had to accept the fact that the so-called relationship, was over and he chose not to participate in the pregnancy!

There was much agony as I did my best to cope with my situation. The agony was compounded by the tormenting fact that I was bringing yet another mouth to feed into my mother's already crowded household. There would be absolutely no support from the absentee father of the child or from me. We were two unemployed teenagers who were too young to be anybody's parents.

Several months after my son's birth, I could no longer stand the mental and emotional pain, thus resulting in a suicide attempt. The love of my beautiful baby boy just wasn't enough. I was convinced that everyone, including my son, would be better off without me. I was also convinced that all the people who didn't love me would be saddened when they discovered my death. Such deceiving thoughts plagued me. I had no clue that God had a plan for my seemingly hopeless life. My only and very selfish desire was to end all consciousness, to escape the torment and pain that saturated my heart and mind day and night.

Falling In Love – How To Be In Love Without Falling

According to Proverbs 23:7, *"As a man [woman] thinks in his [her] heart, so is he [she]."* This scripture is so true! For me, the thoughts that bombarded my mind during that dark time penetrated my heart and shaped my very being for the next few years. My conclusion was that life was not worth living. I had *"fallen"* into a mental and emotional bottomless pit. In my heart, there was no way out except to end my life. I could not see beyond where I was at the time.

I have never felt as stupid as I did when, after the suicide attempt, I awoke in the hospital and looked directly into the distraught face of my mother. I thought, *"Oh no! It didn't work. Now I have to deal with the added shame and embarrassment of what I've done."* Of course the torment continued in a greater degree, and now I was afraid to make another suicide attempt for fear of the same result. Therefore, I felt I had to live miserably with constant torment, pain, even more perceived rejection, which now translated into greater self-hatred.

When my son's father heard about the suicide attempt, he showed up. Yes! I allowed myself to be deceived and allowed him into our lives. It didn't take much because I thought I really loved him though he had hurt me deeply. I conceived yet another son and we married. The marriage was an even deeper *"fall."* Neither of us was ready for marriage nor parenthood, and life was a real mess. We often fought. He was unfaithful and caught in adultery several times.

When our second son died in a tragic accident at the age of 16 months, things grew worse and worse between us. Sometime later, while defending myself in one of our domestic violence incidents, I stabbed him and severely damaged his liver. After that incident it was thoroughly clear that this love/hate relationship could cost one of us our lives. It was the end of the marriage as we went our separate ways. Though we didn't divorce until years later, we never reconciled.

Falling In Love – How To Be In Love Without Falling

At this point in life my heart grew very, very cold toward men, and I measured every man by what I had gone through. There was no ability to trust. I never wanted to *"fall"* like that again. I chose to mask my hurt with promiscuity and a very fast and destructive lifestyle.

Though I was very cold-hearted toward the men who came in and out of my life after that, I was still searching for love and trying to fill a huge void in my heart. Although I secretly vowed never to *"fall"* that hard ever again, I found myself in another destructive relationship. Through this *"fall in love,"* I was introduced to marijuana, cocaine and a lifestyle of illegal activities, many of which led to encounters with the law and even jail time. The second suicide attempt came during this period when, after a huge argument, it appeared the relationship was over. After my first suicide attempt some years before, I was reluctant to try it again for fear it wouldn't work. This relationship, along with the excitement of the lifestyle I was introduced to seemed to motivate me to live. The drugs offered a daily tranquilizing effect that helped me to cope with life in a dysfunctional way. It was at the very least, different!

In any case, after the argument and threat of the relationship being over, I fell into a depressed state and couldn't ward off the overwhelming suicidal thoughts. I had the drugs handy and took enough to fall off to sleep and never wake up. After several days of being unconscious, my partner found me and nursed me back to consciousness. Undoubtedly due to the guilt he couldn't ignore and my lack of self-worth, yet another dysfunctional, love/hate relationship continued, off and on, for several years. It ended when I was led to cry out to the Lord in a moment of desperate hopelessness and sheer disgust for how I was living. The Lord heard my sincere cry, which came from my innermost being, and responded immediately. He came to live in my heart, delivered me from that relationship, the drugs, the spirit of suicide and everything that came with it. He changed my entire life in that moment and gave me new hope, assurance, purpose and the will to live. There were not and never will be any other attempts to end my life. No matter what occurs in my life, because of my relationship with the Lord, it is settled in my heart and mind that suicide is not an option.

"The thief cometh not, but for to steal, and to kill, and to destroy: I am come that they might have life, and that they might have it more abundantly."
(John 10:10)

The evil spirit that drives people to suicide is nothing to play with nor discount. I remember so vividly how that thing spoke to me day and night, tormenting and convincing me that I had no purpose, no future, and no reason to love or live. That demonic spirit was very real then, and is very much alive and thriving in many others today. I wrestled with that thing for years until I was delivered. It all started with my search to fill what I felt was a love void. Little did I know that what I was looking for, no flesh and blood man would ever be able to provide for me.

Yes, the enemy of my soul had a plan to kill me, steal from me, and destroy my life very early on. My first *"falling in love"* experience was a key factor in opening the door to that spirit of suicide that haunted me for so long.

In spite of a difficult young life that I am not proud of along with several failed, so called, love relationships, I was eventually drawn by God to the ultimate love of my life in the person of the Lord Jesus Christ. I learned that the love I had been searching for could only be found in Him. No human being has it.

When Jesus came into my life, I was married to one man *(my son's father)* and living with another. This made me an adulterer and a fornicator. Upon inviting Jesus into my heart, my whole perspective on life, romantic love relationships, and sexual sin was transformed as my mind was consistently renewed with His Word, the Holy Bible. Because of this love relationship, I had the strength to leave the man I was living with at the time, rightfully divorce the man I was still married to, and move on. I eagerly pursued and cultivated my relationship with Jesus Christ, the only Man I had ever known who loved me just the way I was, without condition. I didn't have to do anything in particular or be anyone other than myself. By the way, I didn't know who I actually was at the time or what I should be doing with my life. In any case, He loved me just as I was and I knew it. I learned to love Him through His Word, prayer, worship and the good people He placed in my life in that season.

About two years into my repentance and salvation, I was blessed to be found by an awesome man who loves God and loves me *(Proverbs 18:22)*. We married and the rest is history. We didn't *"fall* in love" as most would think. We believe that God brought us together and we *"grew"* into a love that still stands. With all of the ups, downs, trials, tribulations, and the victories, our love continues to grow deeper and stronger. We continue to learn what unconditional love really is. Yes, there are physical and emotional feelings, but it really boils down to a decision to love and respect each other in spite of emerging shortcomings and becoming inevitably familiar.

I like something that Pastor Michael Todd of Transformation Church (Tulsa, OK) said in a message titled *"The Myth of Dating: Relationship Goals."* He spoke of relationship stages being, *"singleness, then intentional dating (courtship), engagement, marriage (covenant), then comes the real love (1 Corinthians 13:1-13)."*

I agree in that there was infatuation in the beginning, but nothing like the love that manifested after making the marriage covenant and the consummation of that covenant. God blessed us to come together in marriage. Within our approximate nine-month

Falling In Love – How To Be In Love Without Falling

courtship, there was absolutely no physical or sexual intimacy, not even a kiss, prior to our wedding day. I can't say it was easy. I really think it was harder for me to resist than it was for him, but I'm grateful we made it through without *falling* into sexual sin.

I'm sharing in a very transparent way in hopes that you will understand that *"being in love"* is a good thing, but *"falling"* into it, in conformity to society's pattern, is no good. You want to enter such a relationship with your natural and spiritual eyes wide open, a mind that is clear, and a heart that desires to do things the Lord's way. Thanks be to God! He had a plan for the abundant life I now live through His love, mercy and grace.

God also has a plan and purpose for your life. I'm sure that the reason He wanted me to share a very dark part of mine, is to give hope to someone who may be struggling with that very ugly, dark spirit of suicide. You may be struggling with demonic spirits and tormenting thoughts of hopelessness and suicide. It could be through a *"fallen"* relationship of any kind or for any other reason. Whatever the case, please know that God loves you and wants you to be free. Hope and deliverance is available to you just as it was to me through the power of God. *YOU CAN BE DELIVERED TODAY.*

Please pray the following prayer and receive your freedom.

> *God, I come to You as a sinner, I repent of my sins and I ask Jesus to come into my heart right now. Please forgive me for my sins and cleanse me from all unrighteousness. You said that if I don't forgive, I won't be forgiven so I choose, right now, to forgive and release everyone who has hurt or wronged me.*
>
> *I confess with my mouth and believe in my heart that You raised Jesus from the dead. I receive You and all that You have for me now. I ask You to fill me with the Holy*

Spirit with the evidence of speaking in new tongues. I receive all that you have for me right now.

I take authority over and command the spirit of suicide, emotional pain, depression, oppression, rejection, insecurity, confusion and every other unclean spirit to go from me now, in Jesus' Name.

God, lead me to the church and teacher of your choice, so I can learn of You and how You want me to live. I will follow and serve You from this day forward, in the Name of Jesus, Amen! (1 John 1:9; Romans 10:9-10,13; Matthew 6:14-15; Mark 16:17; Matthew 11:28)

If you prayed this prayer with sincerity, wherever you may be and whatever your circumstance, you are now saved and the same Spirit that raised Jesus from the dead is supernaturally dwelling within you this very moment *(Romans 8:10-11)*. God will begin to lead and guide you by the Holy Spirit and you'll never be the same.

Please use the contact information at the end of this book to share your new experience as a result of your repentance and the prayer. We'll send literature to help you continue in your freedom and new life in Christ.

Congratulations! Now, let's get on with the rest of your life!

CHAPTER 3
SEXUAL ACTIVITY - TODAY

One of the main factors that contribute to a *"fall* in love" is desire for SEXUAL ACTIVITY or activity that leads to sexual intercourse! This desire is often misconstrued as *"love"* when much of the time it's simply physical attraction and *lust.* The truth of the matter is sexual activity has NO PLACE other than within the confines of marriage. God created it within that context alone!

Society as a whole has regressed; moreover, it has transgressed by falling away from traditional, biblical values about sexual activity. Biblical values dictate that one man and one woman marry *before* engaging in sexual activity as a means for Godly pleasure and procreation *(Genesis 1:27-28).* Righteousness, in so many cases, is being diminished to pursue meaningless sexual encounters with many partners; the only purpose being lust and fleshly gratification. I've been there, done that! Many have serious issues deriving from these encounters because the activity is so against God's purpose. Heartbreak, emotional impotence and inability to truly love and trust are often results. The effects can be crippling and debilitating for years. Some who fall into the sex trap never recover.

I had the opportunity to speak to a couple of young men about the title of this book and how they viewed love relationships. When I said, *"Falling in Love - How to Be in Love Without Falling,"* they both stopped in their tracks and looked at me as though I had said something foreign. One of them was 21 years old *(we'll call him*

Falling In Love – How To Be In Love Without Falling

Jim). His conversation revealed a carefree view on female companionship. Jim also didn't have much, if any focus on considering God's view on sexual activity. He said that he believed in God and used to attend a church. He also said *"Why go to church when I know I'm going to sin when I leave."* Therefore, he knew that his lifestyle was somewhat sinful. Though Jim was caught by surprise with my conversation, he was sincere in that he had no problem honestly expressing that he was not ready to stop fornicating and would do it whenever he found opportunity and a willing vessel.

We talked about the number of young ladies he had been sexually intimate with. He spoke of how he felt he could actually have sex with a woman and have no mental or lasting emotional attachment whatsoever. I asked a question about his intentions to eventually have a wife, one single romantic relationship at some point in his life. He essentially wasn't interested in that. He was young, virile, handsome and free. The way he saw it, he was just having fun and it was his prerogative to do so at the expense of any young lady's virtue, or lack thereof. After all, this is what people do. At this point in his life, there was no intention to be with any one person for any substantial length of time. After one or more sexual encounters with someone, he was off to the next. I wonder the impact and outcome on the young ladies involved? What state of heart and mind were the young ladies left with? It was so obvious that he didn't have a clue what he was actually doing beyond trying to satisfy his sexual appetite. It was also obvious that some young woman had hurt him at some point, which could be a reason he had such an attitude.

> *"Do you not know that the one who joins himself to a prostitute is one body with her? For He says, "THE TWO SHALL BE ONE FLESH." But the one who is united and joined to the Lord is one spirit with Him. Run away from sexual*

immorality [in any form, whether thought or behavior, whether visual or written]. Every other sin that a man commits is outside the body, but the one who is sexually immoral sins against his own body.
" *(1 Corinthians 6:16-18 AMP)*

Jim, as most don't, didn't realize, he was actually sinning against his *own* body. Only God knows what that could mean for him in his future. He was a prime candidate for some young lady's pregnancy trap and any of the other traps that come with sexual sin and its consequences.

I spoke to him about God's plan for sexual intimacy. I told him that it is designed for marriage alone, not casual encounters of lust *(Genesis 2:18, 24)*. Jim could only shrug his shoulders as if to say, *"Oh well! Que sera, sera!"*

The other young man *(we'll call him Fred)*, 30 years of age, initially had a close relationship with the Lord and regularly attended his local church. His pastor, a very popular preacher with a national television ministry, preaches and teaches the Word of God on all subjects, including sexual sin, in a very simple, easily applicable and effective way.

Fred too was caught by surprise and expressed that he was stunned that I would bring up such a subject, especially at this particular time of his life. He had moved in with a young lady for 2 years and had, just within a few days of our conversation, moved out of the apartment with her. The Lord had been dealing with his heart about how he was living. He and his girlfriend were living as though they were married in a relationship of fornication in spite of the knowledge that it was wrong. Because he was regularly hearing the Word of God, the Holy Spirit was convicting him about his sin. He knew he couldn't comfortably continue in that sinful state. He chose not to keep overriding and ignoring what he knew was right. The conversation we were having may have sealed in his heart that God was pleased with his obedient act of moving out as fruit of true repentance. Matthew 3:8 *(AMP)* says, *"So produce fruit that is consistent with repentance [demonstrating new behavior that proves a change of heart, and a conscious decision to turn away from sin];"* This is exactly what Fred was doing.

On the other hand, Jim, the 21 year old, was in a different place. He wasn't hearing the Word of God. He was steeped into carrying out his own fleshly desires.

I was able to talk to both Jim and Fred for quite a while. Both young men left with plenty of biblical truth to think about. It was obvious that, at least, the younger one (Jim) was steeped in today's societal concepts about sex and superficial relationships. The older one (Fred) seemed to be taking the conversation seriously to heart. After all, the Lord had already dealt with him about his present live-in relationship.

I prayed that the Lord would give Jim space to repent *(Revelations 2:21)* and that He would extend His hand of mercy and grace toward him. I prayed that the Holy Spirit draws him to a place where he can actually see things God's way. That he would turn from the wickedness of his present way of living.

For Fred I prayed that the Lord would continue to strengthen him. That he would walk in righteousness, giving him the ability to resist temptation on every hand. That he would continue to listen to the Holy Spirit and follow obediently and wholeheartedly.

CHAPTER 4
SEXUAL ACTIVITY - YESTERDAY

In times past, the intimacy of a sexual relationship was not synonymous or boasted about within the courtship as it is today. The marriage goal of developing a romantic relationship was apparent. Yes, physical attraction was a factor to reckon with. There was no competition or motivation to prove manhood or womanhood. There was no motivation to define sexuality or lack thereof. You know what I mean, *"if you're a real man or woman, prove it."* Males and females entered into an *"old school"* courtship with a purpose beyond fleshly and superficial motives. There was great effort exercised to avoid a *"fall"* into sexual sin and promiscuity. The goal was to get to know the person and sexual boundaries were respected and not overstepped. There was an unmistakable goal of covenant through Holy matrimony.

> *"Flee sexual immorality. Every sin that a man does is outside the body, but he who commits sexual immorality sins against his own body. Or do you not know that your body is the temple of the Holy Spirit who is in you, whom you have from God, and you are not your own? For you were bought at a price; therefore glorify God in your body and in your spirit, which are God's."*
> *(1 Corinthians 6:18-20 NKJV)*

During the process of getting to the goal of marriage (courtship), there were safeguards in place. There were chaperones, escorts and group outings. The safeguards prevented the possibility of yielding to the temptation to fall into premature sexual intimacy. Because every person is born with a conscience and a sense of right and wrong, they instinctively knew that sex before marriage was immoral *(Romans 1:19)*. People knew there were consequences to falling into the pleasures of sexual sin; however, still some yielded to the temptation to indulge *(Hebrews 11:25)*. There was the risk of illegitimate pregnancy and sexually transmitted diseases *(STDs)*. Moving forward, there was HIV/AIDS. Today COVID-19 could be added to the risk considerations. Even though COVID-19 is not labeled as a "sexually transmitted disease," it can be easily spread through droplets via a cough, sneeze or even breathing in the same space. The Wall Street Journal *(WSJ.com)* published an article on May 7, 2020. It was titled *"Coronavirus Is Found in Semen of COVID-19 Patients."* It stated that, *"The new coronavirus has been found in the semen of infected individuals…raising the prospect that the virus could be sexually transmitted."* I wonder what's next?

Back in *"The Day,"* so-to-speak, physical, mental and emotional dynamics were, and still are, unavoidable. Distractions, interruptions, and sometimes, pure craziness came along with the short-term pleasure of premarital sex. By God's design, believe it or not, having sexual intercourse actually had meaning far beyond the *"one night stand."* It meant, *"I belong to you and you belong to me, only."* The binding effect of sexual intercourse was correct but illegitimate in that, without marriage, it was not God's order though it was His design. He created it to be spiritually, physically, mentally and emotionally binding. It produces such a strong bond that some have committed dangerous acts of crazed jealousy when one party tried to sever the relationship. In my opinion, every violent, *"I can't live without you and if I can't have you no one else will,"* murder or crime of passion, began with at least a perceived *"fall in love."* It undoubtedly escalated with sexual activity at the forefront.

Falling In Love – How To Be In Love Without Falling

> *"...It is good for a man not to touch a woman. Nevertheless, to avoid fornication, let each man have his own wife, and let each woman have her own husband."*
> *(1 Corinthians 7:1-2)*

The sexual act of intercourse is meant to be an intimate, pure, passionate and binding expression of love between husband and wife, not boyfriend and girlfriend. It's a covenant act within marriage that rivals no other. It's how husband and wife procreate and bond with each other over and over and over again throughout the marriage.

I once heard someone say that sex within marriage is a form of spiritual warfare. I couldn't find scripture to verify it, but I tend to believe it. Entering into the act of sexual intercourse itself brings instant unity and the couple is on one accord. Any strife or confusion that was present immediately goes away and stays away at least for the duration of the act. The peace, unity and harmony that follow are phenomenal. I can attest to this because of the strife and confusion we experienced when my husband and I were first married. We often argued and the only time it seemed we were in unity was during sexual intercourse.

Romantic love and sensual sexual activity, with all of the bells and whistles, is a gift from God that He wants us to thoroughly enjoy within the proper context. It's not something we need to *"fall"* into. It's something we should legitimately choose to flow and grow into with sensible spiritual and natural knowledge, wisdom and self-control. This helps to avoid falling onto a slippery, detrimental, emotional slope from which some never recover. Some actually lose their natural lives when what was supposed to be love turns into hate, jealousy, rejection, rage and ultimately murder because of a sexual bond that never should have taken place.

The way romantic love is portrayed in the mainstream media

much of the time, produces conscience-searing, sin-laden imaginations and behaviors that have great influence in our society, especially for the younger generation. Pure, unconditional, *"til death do you part, for richer or poorer, in sickness and in health,"* deeply covenanted love between a man and a woman seems to pale in comparison to superficial, uncommitted, sexually motivated, *"divorce do you part, if we actually marry after shacking up"* conditional type of love.

In times past, sexual connotation was subtly displayed as private and intimate. Today's society displays, *"if it feels good, do it, and do it openly if you like with whomever you desire."* Erotic images depicting men and women as well as same-sex couples, are publicized in the name of love. In reality, perversion and lust *(inordinate desire)* is being openly and seductively flaunted as the acceptable way of giving and receiving love. The goal seems to be to seduce, desensitize and demand inclusive acceptance of blatant sexual sin and perversion as normal, "no big deal" behavior. This totally opposes acceptance and adherence to sexuality God's way between one man married to one woman for life. It totally brings to light what is being relayed in 1 Timothy 4:1-3a.

"Now the Spirit speaks expressly, that in the latter times some shall depart from the faith, giving heed to seducing spirits, and doctrines of devils; speaking lies in hypocrisy; having their conscience seared with a hot iron; "
(1 Timothy 4:1-3)

Do not be deceived; society is actively promoting what is tagged *"new normal."* Overt sexual encounters are common in media and social outlets and no big deal in the eyes of many. You are looked at as strange if you are not actively pursuing sexual gratification in various ways *(masturbation, pornography, sexting, video chats, etc.)* no matter your age or marital status. There are actually some married couples that are consenting to *"an open marriage."* This means that both partners agree that each may have sexual encounters with other people. The Bible calls this adultery. Society calls it *"liberty."* It is a vastly ignorant and deceitful misconception that produces sexual bondage.

> *"Marriage is honorable in all and the bed undefiled, but whoremongers and adulterers, God will judge."*
> *(Hebrews 13:4)*

There was a time when sex on mainstream television was nothing more than an innuendo, if that. You could only see sexual content on paid television. Today, you can see sex and perversion portrayed through something as innocent and simple as a cookie commercial.

My pastor, Pricellious J. Burruss, once shared an analogy concerning the viewing of sexual content through media outlets. I've never forgotten it and it impacted me greatly. The analogy is as follows: Your next-door neighbor contacts you and says, "Hey there! My wife and I will be having sex around 9 pm tonight. You're welcome to watch through the window if you like. We'll leave the curtains open." Wow! It seemed strange at the onset, and I thought, "Who does that?" When it really hit me, it's pretty much what's happening when we willingly engage in viewing sexual content on media.

While I was writing this book, Pastor Pricellious taught a series titled, *"The Sex Series."* She brought out many, if not all of the pertinent, biblical points about sex that any Christian person needs to know and abide by. The messages were life-changing and targeted to all ages. I highly recommend this series, if you desire to please God in your sexuality. It will definitely help you to know and understand how you can possibly keep yourself sanctified and holy, abstaining from any type of sinful sexual activity in spite of the bombardment of society's views.

Falling In Love – How To Be In Love Without Falling

"For this is the will of God, your sanctification: that you should abstain from sexual immorality; that each of you should know how to possess his own vessel in sanctification and honor, not in passion of lust, like the Gentiles who do not know God;"
(1 Thessalonians 4:3-5 NKJV)

"The Sex Series – Part 1" by Pastor Burruss can be viewed on Transformation Christian Church's YouTube channel @ http://youtu.be/HeXuumpFAOc. Believe me, it will help you make good choices concerning sexual activity.

It is important that we all get a clear understanding of what the Bible teaches about sex in order to avoid seduction and a subsequent *fall* into false love. Anytime our government is sanctioning things like same-sex unions, it's evident that our society has taken another wrong turn. This is a far cry from the truth of the Word of God and His ways.

"If a man lies with a male as he lies with a woman, both of them have committed an abomination."
(Leviticus 20:13 NKJV)

"For this reason God gave them up to vile passions. For even their women exchanged the natural use for what is against nature. Likewise also the men, leaving the natural use of the woman, burned in their lust for one another, men with men committing what is shameful, and receiving in themselves the penalty of their error which was due. And even as they did not like to retain God in their knowledge, God gave them over to a debased mind, to do those things which are not fitting;"
(Romans 1:26-28 NKJV)

Not only is mainstream society promoting homosexuality as normal, adult and child pornography, abuse and sex trafficking are being exposed more and more. Some parents are encouraging their children to explore their sexuality at an early age, some even illegally exploiting them for sexual purposes. Children as young as middle school age are dating, having sexual intercourse and getting involved in oral sex, some with the same sex. Children and teenagers are getting involved in threesomes as if this is normal behavior. Many are simply acting out what they have seen and heard at home, at school, and from media outlets.

All of this reminds me of Old Testament times when, *"In those days Israel had no king, so the people did whatever seemed right in their own eyes." (Judges 21:25).* It also reminds me of the people of Sodom and Gomorrah before God destroyed it. *"But the men of Sodom were extremely wicked and sinful against the Lord [unashamed in their open sin before Him]." (Genesis 13:13 AMP)*

I have no stones to throw because I was a prime example of someone who had a seared conscience and did what was right in my own eyes. Because I have no stones to throw, I have wisdom to share with you.

At the time when Christ came into my heart, I was an adulterer and a fornicator. In my sinful state, I thought absolutely nothing of it. It never occurred to me that I should be living any differently. I didn't have a clue as to what true love was all about so I lived in a perpetual *"fallen"* state. When I no longer felt sexually and emotionally charged (in that order), or when I was no longer getting the proper attention from the man I was with at the time, based on my seriously shallow perception of love, I would simply move on to a newer, seemingly fresher one. It didn't take much for me to *"fall"* in or out. All the new one needed to do was show me a little more attention than the previous one and I'd go head over heels into it until the newness wore off; then the cycle was repeated with the next one in line. I was thoroughly ignorant of and indoctrinated with the lack of respect for God's way of being in and maintaining romantic love.

Falling In Love – How To Be In Love Without Falling

After Christ came into my heart, I wasn't really sure what to expect when it came to a romantic relationship. I knew that I couldn't go about it in the same manner that I was accustomed to. I remember being a little confused as to how it was supposed to happen when sexual intimacy was prohibited until marriage. That was unheard of in the lifestyle I came from. I think the term was something like, *"don't buy the cow without tasting the milk."* On the other hand it was said, *"why buy the cow when you can get the milk for free."* Sad to say, many still hold to these clichés. Though some may not necessarily say it, there's no way they would commit to anyone without first experiencing them sexually.

I'm happy to say that my mind was made up that the next time I had sex with anyone, I would be married to that person. At this point, there was no prospect in sight but every now and then my flesh would be provoked to remember my previous days of sexual activity. Of course, the imagination always made it seem that the past was better than it really was. I would feel that I was missing out on something important but this was a lie.

I'm really grateful for the ministry to unmarried people at my local church. The ministry met a couple of times per month and we were taught what the Word of God teaches about being unmarried and in the Lord. I had to learn a different way to handle my sexual appetite, putting it on hold. Thoughts and emotions of the past, as an unmarried believer in Christ Jesus, also had to be cast down consistently.

> *"We are destroying sophisticated arguments and every exalted and proud thing that sets itself up against the [true] knowledge of God, and we are taking every thought and purpose captive to the obedience of Christ…"*
> (2 Corinthians 10:5 AMP)

We, in the United States, are fortunate in that we live in a democracy, a place of freedom of choice. However, if you are a true born-again Christian, no matter what is being presented, promoted, publicized, and depicted as the *"new norm," "politically correct," or "socially acceptable,"* you must choose God's Word and His way of doing things. According to John 17:14, though we live in this world, we are not of it. God's Word on any subject still stands and everyone, believe it or not, will one day give an account to Him.

> *"So then, each of us will give an account of himself to God." (Romans 14:12)*
> *"… Let God be true, but every man a liar….." (Romans 3:4)*

Because of the state of our world and the fact that we live in it, it is paramount to get a good understanding and a consistent working knowledge of real love. We need a true and Godly perspective so as not to *"fall"* into a detrimental trap that pulls people out of the will of God, many times, before you even realize what it really is. Believe me, it's much better than anything or anyone you could even desire for yourself.

> *"Do not love the world or the things in the world. If anyone loves the world, the love of the Father is not in him. For all that is in the world—the lust of the flesh, the lust of the eyes, and the pride of life—is not of the Father but is of the world. And the world is passing away, and the lust of it; but he who does the will of God abides forever."*
> *(1 John 2:15-17 NKJV)*

After my very first "fall in love," a tumultuous relationship and short marriage that ended badly, I resolved in my heart and mind that I would not be hurt again. I learned to detach my emotions. However, deep inside, I was still looking to fill a huge void as I looked for love in all the wrong places. This made me a dangerous woman. I had plenty of encounters of the wrong kind. I tarnished person after person in light of my woundedness. This made me dangerous. As cliché' as it may sound, *"hurt people, hurt people."*

Falling In Love – How To Be In Love Without Falling

It took years for me to climb up that mountain from the despair and relationship hopelessness of one fall after another. Now my desire is to keep others from coming near to the edge of that enticing cliff, avoiding a fall and able to experience the joy of real love. The fall can be avoided with some good Godly wisdom, common sense, obedience to the Word of God, and self-control.

"Now to Him who is able to keep you from stumbling or falling into sin, and to present you unblemished [blameless and faultless] in the presence of His glory with triumphant joy and unspeakable delight," (Jude 24 AMP)

Kacie Starr Long wrote a very interesting blog titled *"10 Reasons Christians Shouldn't Have Sex Before Marriage."* She points out 10 excellent reasons to abstain. There's one reason Kacie pointed out that I had not thought of but is very true. She wrote, *"God has graced you for it."* Once my mind was made up to follow God's way of doing things, I truly experienced His grace to do it. Please read Kacie's blog, especially if you're struggling with the temptation to have sex before marriage. Below is the blog web address:

www.inspiredoverflow.com/single-post/2019/01/18/10-Reasons-Christians-Shouldn't-Have-Sex-Before-Marriage

CHAPTER 5

TYPES OF LOVE
'KNOW THE DIFFERENCE'

A friend of mine from Africa once told me that Americans throw the word "love" around very frivolously. We use it to describe how we feel about people, chocolate, sports, clothing, etc. She said that the word is often used to lie to one another. As I began to pay more attention and monitored how the word was used in different scenarios, I found that she was on the right track to an extent; even down to the reaction icon in the form of a heart that depicts the word on our social media pages. How many times have you clicked on it, only because "like," "wow," "sad," or "laughter" didn't quite describe how you wanted to respond? The heart, depicting, "*love*" is the only option at the time.

My friend was on to something. Thankfully, the Bible speaks of different types of love. Therefore, it's okay to love chocolate; your favorite sports team, your family and your romantic interest all with the same word, as long as you know the difference.

LOVE FOR GOD - CHASHAQ

"Because he has set his love upon Me, therefore I will deliver him; I will set him on high, because he has known My name." (Psalm 91:14 NKJV)

While studying Psalm 91, I ran across this type of love. I believe it should be first and foremost in establishing all types of love. According to Zodhiates' Hebrew/Greek Study Bible Lexical Aids, "Chashaq" is defined *"to be attached, to have pleasure, to delight in. It has the sense of joining together, adhering, cleaving. This kind of love is already bound to its object (God). It can be used to describe man's devotion toward God. It is a love which will not let go."* Wow, I *love* this type. With a love like this for God *"which will not let go,"* anything in life can be overcome and conquered. Yes!

UNCONDITIONAL LOVE - AGAPAO

"...You shall love the Lord your God with all your heart and with all your soul and with all your mind (intellect). This is the great (most important, principal) and first commandment. And a second is like it: You shall love your neighbor as [you do] yourself." (Matthew 22:37-39 AMP)

The Greek word for the type of unconditional love God has for mankind and desires for us all to walk in daily is *"Agape."* When speaking of this type of love, we can refer to the scripture listed above. Agape is the type of love He commands us to have for others no matter who they are or what you think of them. This is the type of love we should be sharing with mankind merely by virtue of being human. This type of love produces mutual respect and random kindness toward one another in a social and moral sense. Interestingly enough, emotions are not primary in this type of love. This is love that operates, without condition, whether you are pleased to love or not or whether you're *"feeling it"* or not.

This is also the type of love that gives us the ability to forgive when we've been offended or wronged.

BROTHERLY LOVE - STORGE

"Be kindly affectioned one to another with brotherly love; in honour preferring one another;" (Romans 12:10)

Falling In Love – How To Be In Love Without Falling

"Now concerning brotherly love, you have no need for anyone to write you, for you have been [personally] taught by God to love one another [that is, to have an unselfish concern for others and to do things for their benefit
(1 Thessalonians 4:9 AMP)

Storge is the Greek word for the family type of love. It fosters natural desire to nurture, protect, honor, respect and to receive the same. Initially, in life, this is a fundamental type of love to experience. It establishes a person within a family. It produces the necessary stability, a sense of belonging, and what I call the "Triple A" principle (Affection, Affirmation, Approval) that is so needed especially at a young age. This type of love should be experienced from conception to birth, into childhood and throughout life within the family.

Often because of the lack of this type of love early in life, perverted views of love can be formed and follow into all relationships. Kind, loving parents and family make a huge difference in your perception of love as you grow up.

If you are a victim of divorce, rape, incest, abuse, abandonment and the like, your view of love could be severely distorted or perverted. Rejection, insecurity and esteem issues develop through such experiences and often cause self-hatred. People carry dangerous, negative emotions into romantic relationships when views on love are distorted. Self-hatred makes it literally impossible to truly love someone else. That hatred will manifest in many negative ways in a romantic relationship.

An abused child lives in confusion about who loves them and if they can even like themselves. These children grow up looking for love. Some feel they can't be loved or give love without being hurt or hurting someone. You know what I mean, *"hurt/hurting people, hurt people."* In turn, child abuse victims can go about life in a very guarded way, unable to trust, especially where a close romantic relationship is concerned.

The good news is that whether you are a product of what is considered to be a good, loving family or an abusive dysfunctional one, the love of God (Agape) covers! This love is always present to keep, repair, restore, renew, revive, and refresh no matter what you've experienced in any stage of life.

I'm reminded of a scripture, Joel 2:25, which was brought to my attention in the first year of my salvation when going through a hard time. It states, *"And I will restore to you the years that the locust hath eaten, the cankerworm, and the caterpillar, and the palmerworm..."* As I took the scripture and meditated on it, it gave me great comfort as I was working through some issues from my past. It helped me to move beyond the thoughts that were tormenting me and trying to hold me back. I pray it will help you as well. God can and will restore no matter what family life was or is like for you.

One day while working at the church office, a young man came in. He was highly intelligent and polite, but also seemed to have some mental challenges. As I began to minister to him, he voiced that his father was abusive for as long as he could remember. He felt he had to leave home to preserve his life, so he did. He had no money and was asking for a ride to get to his sister's house on the other side of town. He mentioned that his sister had also left home at some point because she was unable to get along with their father. This young man's communication style was very standoffish with a fearful demeanor. It was as if he was expecting some type of abuse or rejection from me. However, I was really trying my best to be sensitive and make him feel the love of Jesus. He obviously felt my sincerity, opened up to me and shared his heart. Thankfully, I was able to lead him in a prayer of salvation!

Turns out this man had a little dog with him. He had left him outside. When he brought him in he was very protective and concerned about him. He let me know that the dog was trained and would not soil my automobile, if given a ride. It was so evident that he considered the dog to be his family. He displayed the *"storge"* as well as *"agape"* types of love for the animal and treated him with great care as he brought him in. He treated him with the kind of love and care he desired to receive. It was quite touching to see.

After the heart-warming conversation and praying with him, we were back to the situation at hand. He and his companion needed a ride. I was able to get one of the men from the church to take him and his dog to their destination. He was grateful for the time spent listening to him, the prayer, and the ride. I was grateful to have been used to show love to one who so needed it at that moment and to lead him to the Lord.

FRIENDSHIP - PHILEO

Thirdly, *phileo* or *philia* is the type of love shared within friendship that causes us to bond with others on a platonic (intimate and affectionate, but not sexual) level. This is brotherly or social love. Another Greek translation for this type of love is Philos. It is a generic term for any kind of love between family and between friends. It also speaks of a desire or enjoyment for things like a favorite food or a favorite sport or other activity. The more extended definition hinges on real friendship.

An excellent example of this "Phileo" type of love is one of my grandsons for his best friend. They had gone to preschool as well as kindergarten together. It was so apparent that they were true, platonic friends and established a solid brotherly bond that could last throughout their life span. My grandson talked about his friend all the time and included him in any activity his parents would allow.

The friendship was apparently established in a type of love that was sincere, innocent, and pure. It was quite touching to watch them interact as friends so freely and with such concern for one another. They played together in agreement and sheer enjoyment. Even when they disagreed, they soon rectified the problem between themselves alone, forgave each other and were quickly back to normal.

Many of you have longstanding friendships that were established from childhood and have stood the test of time. Others have formed strong friendships in various stages of life that exemplifies this type of love.

Biblical examples of this type of love can be seen in the relationship between David and Jonathan *(1 Samuel 18:3)*; also Ruth and Naomi even though they were family through marriage *(Ruth 1:16)*. We could definitely look at these relationships noted in the Bible and take note of true loyalty and friendship type of love.

SENSUAL LOVE - EROS

"Then Isaac brought her into his mother Sarah's tent; and he took Rebekah and she became his wife, and he loved her. So Isaac was comforted after his mother's death."
(Genesis 24:67)

Another type of love is *"eros."* It's the word from which we derive "erotic" (sexually arousing and stimulating). It means romantic or physically intimate love. It typically involves physical attraction, passion and sensual love. It denotes sexual desire, physical attraction, and intimacy of the most profound kind.

Eros is meant for romance, passion, sexual intercourse, the most profound spiritual, physical, and emotional intimacy established by God. It is the type of love that, by God's standards, is exclusively shared within a marriage covenant between a man and a woman. It appears that almost every person aspires to obtain this type of love ultimately. Most people seem to desire, anticipate, search for, and wait for this type of love as much if not more than any other. Some even try to make it happen. Many spend their lives in search of it and feel they haven't really lived until it has arrived, thus falling sexually time after time in search of it.

The sexual act by which we were conceived and do conceive is meant to be an erotic expression of intimate love and passion that rivals no other. Again, this was meant only to be enjoyed within the confines of marriage.

⊛ THE LOVE CONGLOMARATE ⊛

A "conglomerate is many different things or parts grouped together to form a whole but remains distinct entities." (Dictionary.com). It occurred to me that every type of love mentioned in the previous paragraphs is a part of the love conglomerate. They should all be developing in any romantic relationship where marriage is the goal.

(Phileo), the friendship type of love, should be developing in a courtship headed for marriage. You're gathering information as you're getting to know the person. Ideally, a potential spouse would become your close friend.

(Eros), the erotic, sexual type of love should only take place on the marriage bed *(Hebrews 13:4)*. Yes, there should be an initial physical attraction and degree of infatuation that is controlled until marriage. Then the Eros can be fully experienced.

(Storge), the family type of love, comes, as you become husband and wife. This is the type of love that will also be shared with the children you'll produce via the intimacy of sexual

intercourse (Eros). Existing children in blended families also experience this love through your marriage union.

(Agape), the unconditional, God kind of love, I believe is the most important. It's hard to say if it should come first, or last. Actually, it's first, last and in between. It's a type of glue that holds all of the other kinds of love in every relationship together. This is the type of love that keeps the marriage together when the honeymoon is over, when difficult times come to try to divide and conquer. It's the kind of love that kicks the door in when forgiveness is needed for a seemingly unforgivable act.

Just thinking of this reminds me of the endless circle that is depicted by a wedding band. There is no beginning and no end and the love, in its various forms, should grow and flow perpetually, year after year. If you ask me, it is exemplary of the infinite God who IS LOVE and placed the desire and capacity for all types of love into the hearts of everyone He creates.

Just think. The very method by which God ordained for us to be conceived and birthed into this earth is by way of an act of love (Eros). A husband and wife come together in a consensual, mutually loving, pleasurable sexual intercourse. Through this act of love, another human being, also created in God's image, is conceived. This fulfills God's command to be fruitful and multiply *(Genesis 1:27-28a)*. This little person who is forming and maturing in the womb, the child has an inherent need to receive and give love (Agape and Storge). This love is needed throughout the pregnancy, at birth, and all through life.

For the majority of human history, everyone was conceived by way of a sexual act, whether consensual or involuntary. In our modern age, medical technology has evolved to provide options such as Invitro Fertilization and Artificial Insemination, for people who are eager to bear and love children yet are unable to do so without some type of physical intervention. Even so, these advances bring forth the conception of a human being who is created in the image of God; someone who must receive love and give love. From the moment life begins, the human spirit seeks to mirror the image of God and His love. This continues throughout every stage of life.

There are some who are conceived through ungodly sexual acts *(rape, molestation, incest, etc.)*. They may enter this world with struggles that are compounded when adequate love is not received before and after birth. The fact that evil was involved in the conception opens the door for negative mental, emotional and spiritual issues from day one. The good news is that God, who is Love, has an uncanny, excellent way of providing love and healing in the most negative, loveless circumstances imaginable. If you are in this category and seem to struggle with giving and receiving love, there is hope.

I pray that as you read this book, God will infuse you with the intrinsic love you may have been missing. I pray that He will give you a fresh, wholesome, holy outlook on how your love needs are to be met. Also, how you can meet the love needs of others in Godly ways.

LUST - AHAB

> *"And it came to pass after this, that Absalom the son of David had a fair sister, whose name was Tamar; and Amnon the son of David loved her. And Amnon was so vexed, that he fell sick for his sister Tamar; for she was a virgin; and Amnon thought it hard for him to do anything to her." (2 Samuel 13:1-2)*
> *"Howbeit he would not hearken unto her voice: but, being stronger than she, forced her, and lay with her. Then Amnon hated her exceedingly; so that the hatred wherewith he hated her was greater than the love wherewith he had loved her. And Amnon said unto her, Arise, be gone. (2 Samuel 13:14-15)*

Falling In Love – How To Be In Love Without Falling

There is one other word I'd like to highlight that translates to the word "love." The Hebrew word for it is *"Ahab."* It's used in the scripture above where it says, *"and Amnon...loved her."* It translates into what means *"pure lust - unusually intense or unbridled sexual desire: lasciviousness."* Another definition references *"an ardent and vehement inclination of the mind and tenderness of affection at the same time."* (Zodhiates' Hebrew Greek Key Study Bible Lexical Aids to the Old Testament).

In the scriptures above, Amnon *lusted* after his half-sister, Tamar. She was beautiful, and his only desire was to have sex with her; so much so that he *"fell sick"* for her. He was deceptive in getting her to a place where he could fulfill his lust. When he was about to rape her, she resisted. She urged him to ask her father for her hand in marriage. This would preserve her honor as a virgin. His intention was not to marry her, but only to fulfill the lust that was driving him. Once he had finished forcing himself on her, he *"hated"* her. He put her out, wanting nothing more to do with her. Tamar's life was forever damaged and desolate. A couple of years later, Absalom, Tamar's brother, killed Amnon. Absalom had to run away, becoming a fugitive for a time after that. Amnon's lust destroyed Tamar's life, ruined Absalom's, and cost him his.

You may be thinking, "That was then, this is now!" Don't get it twisted. There is nothing new under the sun (Ecclesiastes 1:9)! Many men and women alike are still operating in this type of lust every day. They are driven by it until it is fulfilled. Then the object of lust can be hated and lives are damaged, if not destroyed. This is how rape is accomplished.

I bring this out to help someone who is pursuing a love relationship. You may be *"falling* in love," but the other person could be *"falling sick"* with lust. Today, lust is enormous, and sometimes the only motivator for romantic pursuit. This should not be ignored when romantic love is a desire. You must learn the difference between lust and love and what that looks like for you, then for others. Don't be ignorant of evil devices *(2 Corinthians 2:11b)*.

> *"Let no man say when he is tempted, I am tempted of God: for God cannot be tempted with evil, neither tempteth he any man: But every man is tempted, when he is drawn away of his own lust, and enticed. Then when lust hath conceived, it bringeth forth sin: and sin, when it is finished, bringeth forth death." (James 1:13-15)*

It bears repeating. In this media-driven, digital age, we're bombarded with glamorous, lust-promoting images. They give a false depiction of what love should look like. Many of these images promote lustful sexual ecstasy as the ultimate goal. They ignore the God factor, which calls for purity. These images have a significant influence on how people perceive love in a romantic relationship.

In times past, the sexual connotation was subtly displayed as private though alluded to. In today's society, it's *"if it feels good, do it, and do it openly if you like."* This depiction of male and female as well as same-sex couples is publicized in the name of LOVE. Truth is, much, if not most of it is LUST *(inordinate desire)* that is being flaunted as acceptable and normal.

True, committed, *"til death do you part, in sickness and in health,"* deep-rooted love is portrayed as old-fashioned. It seems to pale in comparison to the flashy, superficial, sexually motivated, shallow type of love.

Keep your eyes and ears opened. Take the time to study the different types of love. Whether you could be tempted by someone else's lust (Ahab) or your own, you want to equip yourself to avoid a fall. Take the proper precautions to resist any and all types of lustful temptation.

Falling In Love – How To Be In Love Without Falling

"For this is the will of God, that you be sanctified [separated and set apart from sin]: that you abstain and back away from sexual immorality; that each of you know how to control his own body in holiness and honor [being available for God's purpose and separated from things profane], not [to be used] in lustful passion, like the Gentiles who do not know God and are ignorant of His will;" (I Thessalonians 4:3-5 AMP)

CHAPTER 6
THE GOAL
'HAPPILY EVER AFTER'

In order to live *"happily ever after"* so to speak, you're going to need the proper perspective, propensity and preparation as you're led in life and into true love that doesn't involve a *"fall."* In Jude 24, we see that God is well *"able to keep you from falling. . . . . . ."* as you allow Him to direct your life. A worldly mindset about love will need to be changed. This will require the renewing of your mind. Today's worldview is definitely not good.

"I beseech you therefore, brethren, by the mercies of God, that you present your bodies a living sacrifice, holy, acceptable to God, which is your reasonable service. And do not be conformed to this world, but be transformed by the renewing of your mind, that you may prove what is that good and acceptable and perfect will of God."
(Romans 12:1-2)

If you can conform to the Word of God and His ways, He can lead you into love that will indeed stand and thrive for a lifetime. I really like the God's Word (GW) translation of Romans 12:2. It states, *"Don't become like the people of this world. Instead, change the way you think. Then you will always be able to determine what God really wants—what is good, pleasing, and perfect."*

Falling In Love – How To Be In Love Without Falling

With all the embodiment of love that God is and desires for us to experience, it's no wonder we all seek for what we believe is the ultimate *"in love"* experience and result. That equates to *"happily ever after."*

When Adam was the only person on earth, God said that it was not good for man to be alone. Therefore, He formed a woman *from* Adam *for* Adam, instituting the covenant of marriage between man and woman (*Genesis 2:18*). The union produced help, mutual love, comfort, and companionship. A byproduct of the commanded fruitful multiplication was sexual intimacy and pleasurable fellowship. This would perpetuate for all time and is honorable in the goals for human life and romantic relationships before God.

Everyone born into the earth is God's creation for which He has a plan. Most, if not all, of us are unconscious of the fact that we're raising, grooming, and training our children to ultimately become someone's husband or wife, among other things. Since God directed man to be fruitful and multiply, parenthood is in the plan though some will not experience it for various reasons. However, if you become a spouse and subsequent parent, you too will be responsible for raising, grooming and training someone's spouse as well as someone's parent.

The fact that people move contrary to God's plan doesn't change it. As opposed to the order of marriage, then sex, then parenthood, sex often comes first which countless times results in premature motherhood and fatherhood and consequent parenthood. Marriage may come after, if at all. As God's way is repeatedly disobeyed, this sinful order perpetuates itself. Again, this doesn't change God's original order, which is meant to foster real love, marriage, joy *(not necessarily in that order)* and what society might consider a *"happily ever after"* existence.

What does *"happily ever after"* mean anyway? Wikipedia defines it as, *"a happy ending as epitomized in the standard fairy tale."* In reality, it can't mean the same thing for everyone. What makes me happy may not necessarily make you happy and vice versa. We are all fearfully and wonderfully made by God *(Psalm 139:14)*. We were created with individual and diverse personalities, likes and dislikes. What makes one happy can actually change from moment-to-moment, hour-to-hour, day-to-day, and season-to-season of life with all of its intricacies. In spite of all of this, God's word and order does not change.

In my opinion, *"happily ever after"* equates to being content in whatever state you find yourself in life whether married or unmarried; whether you're in a romantic relationship or not. Philippians 4:11 speaks of *"learning"* to be content in whatever circumstances you find yourself. To take it a bit further, 1 Timothy 6:6-7 (NIV) says, *"But godliness with contentment is great gain. For we brought nothing into the world, and we can take nothing out."* Godliness with contentment brings about great gain, thus, the ability to live "happily ever after" *(so to speak)* no matter what life brings.

The Greek word for *content* in Philippians 4:11, *"autarkes,"* means "self-sufficient, content in the sense of being satisfied because of living in God's content(fulness). This inward sufficiency is as valid in "low times" (suffering) as in 'high times' (temporal prosperity). It means 'sufficiency within' referring to *positive* self-sufficiency (*inward* adequacy) – i.e. that comes through the indwelling power of Christ." *(Hebrew Greek Key Study Bible)*

Life naturally has ups, downs, twists, turns, good and bad times. When you talk about romantic relationships and living *"happily ever after,"* personal contentment is the key factor for both parties individually. Marrying my husband brought to light a powerful reality for me. I realized that, as much as I love him and he loves me, many times we have caused each other unhappiness. There have been times when I didn't like him very much and vice versa, but the deep-seated love remains intact. Because we both have that "inward sufficiency," "God's content(fulness) and the indwelling power of Christ," we've been able to forgive quickly and/or repent, correct things and keep our relationship intact. This has caused us to grow more in unity in the process.

It's amazing to me how we, as humans, make idols out of people, places and things that have limited ability and knowledge to meet our spiritual, mental, emotional and physical needs. We make idols out of money, jobs, children, love relationships, homes, cars, sports, etc. Anything or anyone placed before Almighty God, in essence, is an idol and without even realizing it, you're into idol worship.

Many base happiness on temporary and dissipating things. Most have the delusion that the right person will *"make"* them happy. The truth is if you never learn to be content within yourself with God in the forefront, no person, place or thing will do it. You'll spend your life chasing an illusion.

Learning to be content and full of *real* joy is key to successfully getting through life as people come and go and seasons change. The truth of the matter is that *real* joy comes and remains as a result of obedience to God's word and purpose for your life *(John 15:11)*. Keeping this in mind helps you to adjust and keep your joy intact no matter what happens.

Many times we don't even know what would *really* make us happy. Some think a new car will make them happy. Yes, there may be a time of excitement and initial glee. However, when the notice for the first payment comes there may be a lull in the happiness, right? After driving it for a while, it doesn't have the same *"happy"* effect.

Likewise, you even thought that person you met at the coffee shop was the best thing since mocha latte, only to feel differently after getting to know the individual. The truth is, no person has the capacity to *"make"* and keep anyone happy for as long as it is really needed. You can't even *"make"* yourself happy all of the time because happiness is pretty much based on *"happenings."* Life, in and of itself, is normally pretty mundane and basic. Many are deceived as they try to make things *happen* to break up life's monotony.

A young man may imagine riding up on a fine young lady and magically loving her at first sight like in a fairy tale or some reality TV show. You would kiss her and wake her up to the great Prince Charming that you are, or would like to be. You and she would marry and ride off into the sunset to a dream life. She would be a great cook, housekeeper, and sex toy even after bearing all of your children. She would obey you and answer your beck and call.

A young lady may have imagined being swept off of your feet by a tall, dark, handsome Prince Charming. He would come riding in on a big white horse or, in modern day terms, a BMW, Benz, Tesla, Bentley, etc… He would love, cherish, provide for, romance, encourage, satisfy and protect you for the rest of your days.

In this day and age "Prince Charming" could be riding public transportation. The beautiful young princess' idea of a home-cooked meal could have the word "happy" in front of it, as in McDonald's Happy Meal, if you get my drift. After you wake up from your dream, turn off the television, Internet or whatever device you're viewing, you come to the realization that a true, reality-based love life is not necessarily like the fairytale, movie, reality show, or sitcom you've been engrossed in. Wow, what a rude awakening when you realize that the relationship lacks the media-driven, fairytale expectations you may have desired at the onset! Usually, after a short while, thoughts of, *"This is not what I signed up for"* arise as you realize that you're living your very own reality show. You have to deal with a *real* person, with *real* issues, in *real* life situations. You need some *real*-life guidelines and instructions to follow if you're really going to reach the goal of living *"happily ever after,"* or better still, *"content for eternity"* with the one you desire to spend your love life with on earth.

> *"He who finds a wife finds a good thing,*
> *And obtains favor from the Lord." (Proverbs 18:22 NKJV)*
> *"Oh, how beautiful you are, my beloved! Oh, how beautiful*
> *you are! Your eyes are like doves."*
> *(Song of Solomon 1:15 NIV)*

Gentlemen, when you find a wife, you must realize she *is* your "beautiful young princess," your "beloved" for life, no matter her age. You want to be prepared. You'll need to learn and understand God's view of what a husband is in order to be able and content to love her as Christ loved the church and gave Himself for it *(Ephesians 5:25)*. You'll need to be able to love her as you love yourself, provide for, cover, cherish and lead her and your family in a Godly way *(Ephesians 5:31-33)*. This is the only woman you are to have sexual relationship with. This is not the type of love you want to *"fall"* into and you'll need the Lord's direction *(John 15:5)*.

Some of you may have had Godly fathers who were able to model what a good husband and father look like. Even if you didn't have a good example, God is able to make you the best man and husband ever. His Word clearly defines your role as provider, protector and more. You also have the Holy Spirit and the wisdom of God to help in areas that may not be clearly spelled out in the Word of God. For instance, it's not written in the Word of God who you should marry, although it does say that a "prudent" wife is from the Lord *(Proverbs 19:14)*. It tells you if you find a wife, you've found a good thing *(Proverbs 18:22)*, but doesn't tell you exactly how or where to find her, etc. By trusting and acknowledging God, He will direct you. *(Proverbs 3:5-6)*.

Falling In Love – How To Be In Love Without Falling

"For man did not come from woman, but woman from man; neither was man created for woman, but woman for man."(1 Corinthians 11:8-9 NKJV)

Ladies, you too want to allow God to prepare you to be a suitable "help" and wife to *your* "Prince Charming," the man you marry. You must understand that, in God's eyes, marriage is for life and that's a long time. It goes far beyond the wedding and honeymoon period. It equates to a lot of years living with the same person, having sexual relations with the same person, and becoming familiar with every part of him (good, bad or indifferent). Some things you'll discover you won't necessarily like about each other even though you may have gotten a glimpse of it during courtship. Most, sometimes with much conflict, try to change those things before realizing that the only person you can change is yourself. It's key to ask God for understanding of your place in a marriage and, believe me, it's not what the world's media depicts. From what I read in the Holy Bible, God did not endorse many of the issues of the women's liberation movement that ran rampant in the United States. This is when women began to think they could *"wear the pants"* so-to-speak. At the end of the day, the Christian wife is held accountable to God for how she submits to her husband and how she honors, respects, and helps him in addition to fulfilling other things. *(Ephesians 5:22-24)*

Proverbs 31:10-31 is a biblical model of a great wife. Her husband trusts in her, she takes care of her children and household, has her own business with employees, gives to the poor, operates in wisdom, etc... I would say she is definitely walking in the supernatural in handling all that is recorded there. Though this is a good model to aspire to, you may not have all of that going on. Actually the Lord may not be requiring all of that of you. Just trust and obey Him to be all you need to be in Him!

Falling In Love – How To Be In Love Without Falling

You too can be taught to be a good, godly wife, even if you didn't have a good example as you were growing up. It would be wonderful if all could be learned prior to entering into marriage. Unfortunately, or fortunately, depending on how you look at it, much of what is learned about being a godly wife happens by trial and error after the *"I do's."* Its all a part of the *"happily ever after"* or *"content for eternity"* process experience.

When a man and a woman are able to at least *begin* to view romantic love and life in general, in the way God intended, you are on your way to living a life of contentment.

Unfortunately, many who are unmarried, especially ladies, live life in waiting and expectation, primarily for a man and a wedding day. The idea of an elegant wedding actually becomes an object of worship or an idol in a sense. You talk about it, dream about it, believe God for it, and make decisions and choices based on the expectation of it. The idea is viewed as the *"be-all and end-all"* that will solve all your problems. Many have a list written someplace as to the type of mate and wedding you desire, praying about it often. Some go as far as planning out the wedding and collecting items for the occasion for years. However, there are no real plans beyond the wedding day and imagined honeymoon. There was one young lady I was privileged to disciple for some time after she accepted Christ as Savior. Every conversation we had eventually came down to her desire to have a romantic relationship and be married. It took some convincing for her to eventually accept that she was already married to the Lord of Hosts *(Isaiah 54:5)* and as she delighted herself in Him, He would see to it that she would receive what and who was best for her.

> *"Delight yourself also in the LORD, And He shall give you the desires of your heart. Commit your way to the LORD, Trust also in Him, And He shall bring it to pass."*
> *(Psalm 37:4-5 NKJV)*

Falling In Love – How To Be In Love Without Falling

There are cases where people never marry or don't even desire to marry. Jeremiah, a powerful prophet who was called by God before he was even formed in his mother's womb (Jeremiah 1:5), was instructed by God not to marry and have children. It is thought that this was due to the controversial lifestyle he was called to and the perilous times and place in which he lived.

There is one popular gospel singer, who shall remain nameless, who has never been married and publicly announced that he has no desire to ever be married. I'm sure some would say there was something wrong with that. However, he could truly be delighting in the Lord and the single lifestyle he is so content with, and without the element of sexual sin.

Marriage is indeed an honorable institution *(Hebrews 13:4)* that most want to experience, but what if it's not in the plan for you? There was a beautiful young, single lady who attended our local church for a while. She was a faithful Christian who loved the Lord and served Him well. At some point in life she had chosen to live a celibate lifestyle and wait until God blessed her with a mate. I believe she was not in a romantic or sexual relationship. One Sunday morning, she went for a run in the park before church. She never returned because she passed out and went to be with the Lord that very day. Just think, she left this earth suddenly, without a husband and without sexual intimacy in a marriage. Did being without a husband mean that she didn't live a life of contentment? I believe she lived a full and satisfying life without being in a romantic relationship. She is now experiencing the ultimate *"contentment"* for eternity because of her relationship with the Lord prior to her death - absent from the body, present with the Lord *(2 Corinthians 5:8)*.

How would you live your life, if you knew marriage was not in the picture? Would it be the end of the world? No! It's not wise to spend your single, unmarried life just waiting to be married, looking for Mr. or Mrs. "Right" around every corner. It's too easy to be deceived that way and often leads to hooking up with Mr. or Mrs. "All Wrong." It's best to spend your life waiting upon the Lord, serving Him and delighting yourself in Him. In Matthew 22:37 Jesus said, *"Love the Lord your God with all your heart and with all your soul and with all your mind."* Also, Isaiah 40:31 says, *"But they that wait upon the LORD shall renew their strength; they shall mount up with wings as eagles; they shall run, and not be weary; and they shall walk, and not faint."* When you learn to love the Lord this way, wait on Him and His timing in everything to the best of your ability, you can be content whether and when you marry or not. You *will* be living *"happily ever after."*

Personally, I believe that the Lord not only gives the command to *"love Him"* but He actually infuses you with the ability to do it immediately when He is sincerely asked to come into your heart. The love grows and grows as you cultivate the relationship.

CHAPTER 7
THE CLOSE CALL

I learned early on in my Christian walk, before remarriage, that as I work at delighting myself in the Lord, learn to love and cultivate my relationship with Him, my desires will line up with His desires for me. Before I gave my life to Christ, I had perverted ideas of what a romantic relationship should be like. Whenever I was in a relationship, sex was inevitable based on the fleshly way we related to each other. There seemed to have been no relationship without it and sometimes the only real type of intimate communication. As previously stated, I had been living and sleeping with one man, yet married to and separated from another. What a mess! I was practicing the sin of fornication *(sex outside of marriage)* and adultery *(sex with someone other than the one presently married to)*. I didn't have a clue of what God desired for me where this was concerned. Like most who don't know God, I never gave a thought as to what and whom He wanted for my life. I just did things the way I thought they should be done. Believe me, I suffered much for it. It was self-destructive and destructive to others. After I gave my life to Christ, one of the first things I realized was that God's desire for me was to *"flee from sexual sin"* according to 1 Corinthians 6:18. His desire for me was not to keep *"falling"* into sexual sin.

When Jesus came into my heart, and I was led to my local church, I was taught the Word of God. Little by little, a transformation was taking place and I was able to do *whatever* was necessary to live a holy lifestyle and walk in freedom from sexual sin.

> *"Prove by the way you live that you have repented of your sins and turned to God." (Matthew 3:8 NLT)*

My proof of true repentance was to end the relationship with the man I was not married to. I then moved out of the apartment we shared that was in my name and into a single room in a friend's home.

The next step was to divorce the man I had been separated from in my early years. I went to an attorney who told me I would have to locate him. I didn't know how to find him. I was instructed that if I placed an ad in an obscure newspaper and he didn't see and respond to it, the divorce could be obtained without him being present. I placed an ad in a small newspaper. Wouldn't you know it? He actually saw the ad and contacted me! Then a different battle of confusion raged within me. Because I was a babe in Christ, my heart was very tender and open with desire to do whatever I thought the Lord wanted me to, even if it meant going back to an abusive, alcoholic, drug infested, relationship. At the time I had childlike, or shall I say, naive faith. I wanted to believe that the Lord would deliver him, just like He delivered me. We could reconcile and live *"happily ever after."* I was bombarded with confusing thoughts but prayed for the Lord to show me what I was supposed to do. Why had we been separated for so long and neither of us ever even attempted to get a divorce? Maybe we're supposed to be together. Surely this was a *"sign from God,"* right? Wrong! In my opinion, we were never supposed to be married in the first place.

Falling In Love – How To Be In Love Without Falling

After he contacted me, I took the bus and met him at a local restaurant. He looked very bad and was very shaky. We talked and I shared with him that I was saved now and just wanted to do the right thing because we were still married. To my surprise and for the first time ever, he mentioned a scripture to me. He said, *"the Bible says in 1 Corinthians 7 that you should be reconciled to your husband."* Mind you, the whole time I had known him, he had never gone to church or even mentioned anything slightly spiritual to me that I can remember. Now, he actually knows what the Bible says about marriage, and he quoted if off the top of his head, just like that! Was he saved? How did he know this? I was thrown for a loop and more confusion set in. I didn't know what to do!

In the meantime, I couldn't wait to get to my Bible so I could study the scriptures he had quoted. We got through the conversation and I asked him to drop me off at home since I didn't have a car. We sat in his car and talked for a few minutes. He reached over and touched my hand. When I turned to look at him, I remembered what he used to look like, how handsome he was to me when we were in school when I *"fell in love"* with him and subsequently into sin. My mind began to drift back to those days. His face seemed to transform to that handsome, boyish image. An overwhelming sexual heat came over me. Suddenly it was as if someone actually opened the car door and snatched me out. Without a word, I ran up the stairs and fell onto my bed in prayer. There was a serious battle raging on the inside of me as confusion and emotions raged. This was my first experience with real spiritual warfare, and I wanted to be touched sexually. I was fighting so many thoughts and emotions I could hardly stand it. I don't know if it was a demon spirit or my flesh, but I thought, *"He is your husband. You could actually legally have sex with him. Go ahead. It's been so long and it won't be sin this time. You're still married."* I battled with my thoughts until I drifted off to sleep fully dressed. When I awoke the next morning, I felt like I had actually been in a physical fight. I was tired and groggy with sore muscles.

> *"To the married I give this command (not I, but the Lord): A wife must not separate from her husband. But if she does, she must remain unmarried or else be reconciled to her husband. And a husband must not divorce his wife."*
> *(1 Corinthians 7:10-11 NIV)*

What he said to me about the Bible was prevalent in my mind, so I looked it up. When I opened my Bible to it, I was stunned! I took it as an instruction from the Lord that I should reconcile with him. However, the lust had somehow subsided for a time and it now made me sick to think of being with him again. My spirit was disturbed and without peace. I was struggling and badly confused for days. Later, I learned that God is not the author of confusion *(1 Corinthians 14:33)*.

According to Proverbs 11:14, *"Where no counsel is, the people fall but in the multitude of counselors there is safety."* Therefore, I went for spiritual counsel and a simple question was posed to me: *"Vanessa, do you really believe that the Lord would deliver you from a life of addiction and bondage and then put you right back into it with someone who is obviously still involved in that lifestyle?"* I shared how my ex-husband had quoted from 1 Corinthians 7:10-11 to me. It was shared with me that Satan quoted God's word to tempt Jesus in Matthew 4. Therefore, it could also be used to deceive me.

After that session, I really knew in my heart of hearts what I needed to do. The problem was that I was still struggling with my flesh, and I wanted to have sex. I was resisting the urge, but the thought just kept coming, *"he is still your husband. You can legitimately have sex with him."* All of a sudden, the idea of being with him didn't seem so bad after all.

Falling In Love – How To Be In Love Without Falling

One day, when I came home from work, my ex-husband was sitting in his car, waiting. I stood outside the car and let him know I was going through with the divorce and into the rest of my life without him. He very cunningly said, *"If you were really saved, you would come home with me right now. The Bible says you should be reconciled to me. I'm your husband."* In a moment of pride concerning my salvation, along with that fleshly desire to have sex, I got into the car. I said, *"Yes, I'm really saved. Let's go."* He didn't say another word as he drove off with me, and there was a weird, awkward silence. A few minutes into the drive I turned to look at him. There was a sinister grin on his lips and his countenance looked evil. It was almost as if I heard him say, *"I've got you now."* All of a sudden a fear I can't explain came over me and there was no doubt that this was wrong, wrong, wrong! I turned, looked at him and screamed with great authority, *"If you don't let me out of this car, I'm going to jump out. Turn this car around and take me home."* Without a word, he turned around and drove me home, both of us looking straight ahead. Still with no words spoken, I jumped out of the car and confidently went into the house. That was the end of the story. That battle was over and a peace overshadowed me. I continued with the divorce and he didn't even show up in court. I had total peace after that and felt that a major spiritual and physical victory had been won. Glory to God!

Sometime after that, I had a vision of myself being chained to a chair in the basement of his house. I had been rescued from a terrible *fall*. Thank God for Godly counsel and the power of the Holy Spirit who leads us into all truth *(John 16:13)*!

God showed me much grace and step by step, unraveled the mess I had been in for years. I was so free and totally understood and accepted that sexual impropriety was no longer an option. My heart was now fixed to wait until I was married again to have any sexual contact. I was determined to avoid a *fall* in this area of my life and to please the Lord however I could. Though this was the case, there was another door the Lord had to reveal to me that had to be closed.

About a year into my salvation, the young lady who had so graciously allowed me to come live in her home when I moved out of my apartment, backslid. She started living as though she wasn't a Christian at all. Her home was the perfect place for that season, however after she backslid she began inviting men into the home, smoking, drinking, doing drugs, and obviously not following Christ anymore. Her lifestyle change began to cause temptation for me. If I wanted to keep my salvation intact, I had to move out. I found a Salvation Army facility and moved into a one-room apartment.

The Salvation Army building I moved to housed several floors of men and a couple floors of women. I was truly saved, following Christ, and thought I was being a great witness for the Lord as I shared Jesus often and invited them to church. I found myself drawn to the men in the building. I convinced myself that the women didn't really want what I was offering. Well, low and behold, one day as I was walking past one of the ladies to get to one of the men, I heard in my spirit, *"You are a flirt!"* It hit me pretty hard as I began to think about, not so much what, but how I was doing what I was doing. Yes, I was witnessing Jesus Christ to the men and inviting them to church, but in the process I was receiving a type of attention that I used to receive in my previous lifestyle when I would openly flirt with men for the purpose of using them for financial gain or sexual gratification. Oh my! What an eye-opener! It caused me to repent and change my ways immediately. I started witnessing to the women much more and spent less time in extended conversations with the men in the building. God was working on me bit by bit. It was all for the good as I had much to learn about myself and how God would have things done. If I would adhere, I would be kept from a *fall*.

CHAPTER 8
THE MARRIAGE BLESSING

After my deliverance from the desire for male attention and a flirtatious spirit, I threw myself into my work and church activities. I worked in the administration office of my local church and faithfully served in several ministries. There were many men who came through the ministry who I had to serve and interact with. No longer a flirt, by the way I carried myself, most men were reluctant to approach me for any reason other than ministry business. I kept myself covered from the neck down and had no desire to give even the appearance of flirting. I went from one extreme to another.

One day I had a very sobering revelation after a man approached the desk where I worked. He seemed almost afraid to speak with me and it bothered me. After I pried out of him what he needed and gave him the information, he left the building. Not that it was a focus, but a passing thought came to mind, *"You're never going to get married because all of the men are afraid to talk to you."* It made me sad and I thought of some other encounters I had with others who seemed to be afraid to approach me as well. As I got up from my desk and walked into a storage closet, I heard quietly in my spirit, *"But the one I have for you won't be afraid to talk to you at all."* This encouraged me, and I went about my work forgetting the whole scenario.

Falling In Love – How To Be In Love Without Falling

Some time later, a man came and joined one of our Morning Prayer meetings. As we closed in prayer, we all joined hands, and I heard in my heart, *"this is your husband."* It frightened me and I abruptly broke the prayer circle and quickly went downstairs to my office to work, not knowing what to say or do. It was very distracting. Soon he came downstairs and stopped at my desk, which made me very nervous because I still didn't know what to say. He immediately started talking to me with absolutely no apprehension whatsoever. He talked, asked questions, talked, asked questions, and then talked some more. Anyone who knows my husband knows exactly what I mean. He is the type of person who has never met a stranger. Finally, I had to ask him to leave so I could get to work.

The next thing I know, he was regularly attending the church and showing up often to talk to me. He and one of my pastors began to take short rides together, having conversations, some of which were undoubtedly about his intentions concerning me. Soon after, he asked me out to a basketball game he was officiating. You would have thought I was a teenager due to the nervousness I experienced. I did say yes, but I wanted to do this thing right. When he came to pick me up for the date, I grabbed a friend who lived in the same building where I lived to go with me on the date. He seemed puzzled when I walked out of the door with my friend and we both got into the car with him. We made it work, had a great time, and it was the beginning of our courtship for marriage.

Our courtship was difficult, to say the least. Why? Because neither of us had ever been in a romantic relationship where sexual activity was not a primary and major factor. This time, we were both saved, serving the Lord, very much into the Word of God in the Bible, and out of sexual sin. I had no desire to *"fall"* back into it. Very careful and prayerful to keep ourselves out of compromising situations where we could be tempted, there was no petting, hugging, kissing or similar activity. I believe it was more difficult for me than it was for him. He didn't know at the time, but there was one time after leaving a tennis court, where a simple touch from him to my bare shoulder while wearing a sleeveless t-shirt, ignited my body. The warmth of his hand aroused me to the point where I simply had to run away and gather myself. The Bible says in 1 Corinthians 6:18 to *"flee sexual immorality."* I found myself running away more times than I'd like to admit.

Thanks be to God, we made it through our relatively short, nine-month courtship without *falling* into sexual sin! We got to know each other without sexual intimacy, at least as much as we could without living together. We did not *"fall"* in love. We enjoyed each other and believed God brought us together as our love began a growth process.

It was much different than all other love relationships from my past. Our very first kiss was enjoyed at our wedding after our pastor said, *"I now pronounce you husband and wife. You may now kiss the bride."* I must say that it was the very best kiss I can ever remember, as was the sexual experience. I trusted God that if He indeed brought us together, coming together as one was going to be phenomenally pleasurable. It was and still is.

After the wedding night and honeymoon, the real work of growing into a loving, committed marriage began. The adventure of *"becoming one"* was under way. At the penning of this book, we have been married for 28 years, and our love has grown deeper and deeper from year to year. We have honored our covenant and worked at *"growing in love"* without *"falling"* into a divorce or loveless existence no matter what we've had to go through.

TO BE IN LOVE
WITHOUT FALLING

CHAPTER 9
GROW IN LOVE WITH GOD

"And you shall love the Lord your God with all your heart, and with all your soul (life), and with all your mind (thought, understanding) and with all your strength."
(Mark 12:30 AMP)

The first thing to consider in how to BE IN LOVE WITHOUT FALLING is your relationship with God through Jesus Christ. You must be progressively growing in your love with Him! This should be your number one priority with no other purpose than to get to know and love Him intimately. Though other relationships like family, friends, love interests, and any other relationship in your life is important, your relationship with God must come first. It must be foremost in your heart and mind. All others should only be secondary at best!

It's amazing how much weight and attention is given to human relationships, especially when romance is in the picture. You anxiously wait for calls, texts, posts, etc., immediately acknowledging, reading, responding, and thoroughly enjoying the communication. In the proper perspective, this is rightfully so because God created us to be social, relational beings. The same type of excitement and energy, if not more so, should go into developing and cultivating the relationship and communication with the Lord. You should be eager to read His Word in the Bible and eager to commune with Him through regular prayer and worship. You should be excitedly waiting for His every communication throughout your days. You should practice to get good at hearing and recognizing His voice and hand in everything, and acknowledging Him always *(Proverbs 3:5)*. You want to get to know His voice so that no other voice will be able to entice or lure you into deception *(John 10:27)*.

You must establish and deepen your love for the Lord *(Matthew 22:37-39)*, to learn of Him *(Matthew 11:28-30)*, and to watch and listen for His cues and directions. His Holy Spirit, who comes to live in you when you ask Him into your heart, will guide you into all truth and show you things to come in your life as God sees fit *(John 16:13)*. As your love and relationship grows, you will be able to recognize the leading of the Holy Spirit in countless and diverse ways in your daily life.

It is so important to have your love for God intact at all times! Realize that He loves you more than you can imagine, and everything you will ever need flows from and through Him. Keeping Him as your main focus will help keep your perspective clear concerning all of your relationships.

As you deepen your relationship with Him, your desire to please Him will progressively increase. As you delight yourself in Him, there will be no desire to deliberately do anything that would violate that relationship. Therefore, when you aspire to enter into any other relationship, your desire will be that it lines up with your relationship with Him. Delighting yourself in Him will get you the desires of your heart *(Psalm 37:4)*. The blessing is that as you consciously delight yourself in Him, your desires will begin to subconsciously line up with His desires for you. How perfect is that?

Because of your love for Jesus, not only will your desires begin to change for good, you will want to know what He wants you to do according to His commandments and ways. John 14:15

states, *"If you love me, keep my commandments."* Keeping His commandments will mean learning then doing His commandments. The word "commandment" has a somewhat stern connotation. According to 1 John 5:3, *"For this is the love of God, that we keep His commandments: and His commandments are not grievous."* This means they are not painful, oppressive or restrictive. They are not difficult or too hard to obey. I love the fact that whatever He has commanded that we do, He has already given us the ability to obey. Your diligence and desire to love Him and obey will only benefit you in a good way.

Many good things as well as adverse things happen in life. Things happen that cause hardship and trouble. (Job 14:1 AMP) *"Man, [meaning mankind which includes woman] who is born of a woman, is short-lived and full of turmoil.").* Trouble is guaranteed as a part of life. Jesus said in John 16:33 that trouble is a part of being in this world, but that we should still have joy because He has overcome the world. If you can love God enough to believe what has been written in His Word in the Bible and actually live by it, trouble won't seem so daunting and difficult to work through. In this way of life, no matter what the situation, no matter who comes, who goes, or what happens, you can weather it and still maintain joy.

The truth is, people and various relationships do come and go in life for a variety of reasons. There's life, there's death, there's desertion, and relocation, divorce and other reasons people come and go from your life. Whatever the season or time you may be with people, the Word of God in the Bible assures that the Lord will NEVER leave nor forsake you *(Deuteronomy 31:6; Hebrews 13:5)*. He has promised to be with you in good and bad times no matter who or what happens *(Isaiah 41:10)*. Even though there are times when you might leave Him, in a sense, He is the ONLY ONE who will never leave you for any reason. You must come to realize that He is the one who helps you through every situation and season, good or bad. He's the one who will keep you from falling. He is also the only one who is able to pick you up if you do happen to fall, no matter how many times *(Proverbs 24:16a)*.

Once you realize the fact that He will never leave you nor forsake you, you determine that it is well worth establishing and continually deepening your relationship with Him. He is always present and available to help in times of need *(Psalm 46:1)*. He is also always available in times when you don't think you need His help, if there is such a time. Loving Him *IS* the end-all and be-all and an awesome foundation for all relationships! Loving Him, learning of Him and listening to Him, with the intent and determination to do what He says, are key in identifying and subsequently living in a real love relationship. This is where your contentment, growth and fruitfulness lie in all areas of life at all times. You must realize that no one ever has or ever will love you like or as much as He does. I've heard it said that He loves you enough to give you what you need, which many times may not necessarily be what you feel you want. He knows what and who is best for you, and He has no problem communicating that to you as you learn to listen and obey Him. You must realize that He does all things well, and there is no error in Him *(Mark 7:37)*.

When I had my life-changing encounter with the Lord in 1989, I was supernaturally infused with love for Him. It was and still is a type of love I had never known. There was an immediate exchange that took place. The exchange was my pathetic way of living, thinking and loving in exchange for the life and love Jesus died for me to have. I remember how tears flowed for days as my repentant heart melted with gratitude at the overwhelmingly powerful and supernatural knowledge of His love for me. I actually felt His love and knew that through it, He had delivered me from drug, alcohol, and nicotine addictions. He also delivered me from a fallen, toxic, unsuitable love relationship and sinful lifestyle. He manifested Himself and His love to me when I knew nothing. I became a part of Him as He came to live inside of me.

> *"I will give you a new heart and put a new spirit in you; I will remove from you your heart of stone and give you a heart of flesh." (Ezekiel 36:26 NIV)*

Before my encounter with the Lord, my heart was hard and stony. It was so broken in pieces and perverted. God knew that I needed a new one. That very day when I cried out with a desperate and sincere cry, He changed me and put a new heart and a new spirit within me. I was in love with Him from that moment on and there was no "fall" involved. It was a very sweet, gentle flow into it. There was immediate gratitude and a deep desire to learn who He was and about the new life I was entering.

> *"Come unto Me, all you who labor and are heavy laden, and I will give you rest. Take My yoke upon you and learn from Me, for I am gentle and lowly in heart, and you will find rest for your souls." (Matthew 11:28-29 NKJV)*

The love I was clearly experiencing paralleled no other that I had known. It was pure and holy and came with an assurance that no one could touch or change. It brought immediate joy, happiness and amazing hope for my future. It made Jeremiah 29:11 *(NIV)* real for me, *"For I know the plans I have for you, declares the Lord, plans to prosper you and not to harm you, plans to give you hope and a future."*

I'll never forget the joy I was experiencing through all of the tears and the new things that were supernaturally occurring. I was so happy and was able to make the decision to surrender the earthly, superficial love in my life in exchange for the deep, but simple agape love that had so quickly and thoroughly overtaken me. Though somewhat strange, unfamiliar and difficult, at the same time it was easy to walk in the steps He was laying out for me because of what He had done in my heart. The excitement and anticipation for my new life was nothing short of amazing and empowering! I wanted to know Him, His commandments and His will for me. More importantly, I wanted to follow Him to the best of my ability.

Since God is no respecter of persons *(Acts 10:34)*, you too can experience the excitement and anticipation of His unconditional love for you! You can experience the excitement, anticipation and ability to love Him with all your heart, soul, and strength *(Mark 12:30)*. When you sincerely repent of your sins and ask Jesus Christ to come into your heart, He gracefully infuses you with the ability to love and obey Him. He also fills you with the desire to know Him. He would never instruct you to do something that He has not equipped you to do. Your responsibility is to dive into communicating with Him through prayer. This simply entails spending time talking to Him and listening, becoming familiar with how He communicates with you. You'll need to develop a habit of reading and studying His Word, the Holy Bible. There are Bible apps where you can listen to the scriptures being read to you, some with dramatization. I really like this method because you can listen to a particular verse or section of scripture over and over again. This really helps with meditation and memorization of the Word of God!

> *"This book of the law shall not depart out of thy mouth; but thou shalt meditate therein day and night, that thou mayest observe to do according to all that is written therein: for then thou shalt make thy way prosperous, and thou shalt have good success." (Joshua 1:8)*

> *"Study to shew thyself approved unto God, a workman that needeth not to be ashamed, rightly dividing the word of truth." (2 Timothy 2:15)*

Falling In Love – How To Be In Love Without Falling

Personal time is so important in establishing your love relationship with your First and most important Love. This is the time when your prayer, praise and worship life is developed. As you study and learn of Him, you'll learn how to pray according to the scriptures.

> *"Put Me in remembrance: let us plead together; declare thou, that thou mayest be justified."*
> *(Isaiah 43:26)*

Until you learn some of what is in the Word of God in order to pray according to it, your simple heartfelt requests are definitely heard and answered. When I first asked Jesus into my heart, I knew nothing about the Word of God, the Bible, except maybe the Lord's Prayer *(Matthew 6:9-13)*. Nonetheless, I talked to God daily. He kept amazing me. There were many times when I would just think of something that I wanted or needed. He would provide it, and I knew it was He. This caused me to spend more time praying whatever I knew to pray and seeking knowledge of His Word. It seemed as if the more knowledgeable I became of Him and His Word, I had to learn to be more strategic and specific about my prayers. Answers didn't seem to come quite as easily or quickly. Later, I realized that the Lord was helping me to increase my faith in Him and rely on the truth of His Word.

Roman 12:3 says that God has given everyone *"the measure of faith."* In my opinion, this is enough to believe and accept Jesus as Savior and give our lives to Him. After accepting Him into our hearts, it's up to us to increase that measure. Romans 10:17 says, *"Faith comes by hearing and hearing by the Word of God,"* and *"without faith, it is impossible to please God" (Hebrews 11:6)*. He let me know early on that He knew that I was seeking Him as well as delighting myself in Him *(Psalm 37:4)*. This caused increase in my faith to seek Him more and more.

Falling In Love – How To Be In Love Without Falling

You too will need to establish a habit of seeking Him by listening to sound biblical teaching, in addition to reading and studying His Word. In your prayers, ask the Lord to lead you to the church and pastor/teacher of His choice for you. This is extremely important in your growth and development process. To bring God in remembrance of His Word, you'll have to learn what's in it and how to apply it in prayer and to life's everyday situations.

CHAPTER 10
ESTABLISH YOUR LIFELINE

PRAYER

*"I call on You, my God, for you will answer me;
turn your ear to me and hear my prayer." (Psalm 17:6)
"Pray without ceasing.." (1 Thessalonians 5:17)
"….men ought always to pray, and not to faint." (Luke 18:1)*

Prayer is a huge part of your lifeline, especially praying according to God's Word. It is *THE* most important part of *"being in love with God"* and developing your relationship with Him. More so than any human, He should be the one you talk to all throughout the day. First Thessalonians 5:17 tells you to *"pray without ceasing."* Luke 18:1 tells you that you should *"always pray and not faint"* in doing so. Philippians 4:6 tells you to *"be anxious about nothing, but to pray about everything."* Prayer is how you make your requests known to God and obtain peace, as you trust Him to show you what to do as He works things out. This refers to romantic relationship issues as well. Your commitment to prayer, effectively communicating with God daily, can be the key to preventing a *"fall"* into a detrimental love relationship. It can also be the key to your *"rise"* into the most fulfilling love relationship you could ever imagine.

I recommend a book titled, *"Prevailing Prayer"* by Pastor Teresa Thiongo' of Kitale, Kenya. There are profound but practical principles noted in the book that will open your eyes to the importance of your prayer life.

There is another book I recommend titled, *"Prayers That Avail Much" (Commemorative Gift Edition)*, by Germaine Copeland of Word Ministries, Inc. This book is a compilation of three volumes of prayers for practically every situation and relationship. The prayers are neatly organized in sections and include the scriptures pertaining to each prayer. It's a great way to learn how to pray according to God's Word.

Prayer in its simplest form is *"conversing with God."* You can talk to Him in the simplest form you know. You should also expect for Him to talk back. The goal is to have a love relationship with Him to where you are in continual, consistent, and two-way communication. This is key in preventing mistakes that cause you to *"fall."*

> *"And be not conformed to this world: but be ye transformed by the renewing of your mind, that ye may prove what is that good, and acceptable, and perfect, will of God.*
> *(Romans 12:2)*

Study of the Holy Bible is another important part of your lifeline. When you begin to study His Word, it will help you enhance your relationship with Him. Your mind will be renewed, your way of thinking will change, and you will be transformed. With a renewed mind, you can have knowledgeable conversations *(prayer)* that are according to His will. You won't be praying all over the place, ignorantly asking for things that are contrary to His Word and His will. You won't be praying in the dark, so to speak. Psalm 119:130 (NKJV) states, *"The entrance of Your words gives light and; it gives understanding to the simple."*

> *"All scripture is given by inspiration of God, and is profitable for doctrine, for reproof, for correction, for instruction in righteousness: That the man of God may be perfect, thoroughly furnished unto all good works."*

Falling In Love – How To Be In Love Without Falling

(2 Timothy 3:16-17)

The supernatural power that is present as you read and study His word can open your eyes and equip you to handle all aspects of your life. There are things that you will pray about that are not necessarily written verbatim in the Bible. However, because of your love relationship with God, He will give you direction. Things like who to marry, where to live, what job to take, whom to connect with for various reasons, etc., will not be written there. Nonetheless, what *is* written can help you to determine His will and the direction you should take. For instance, there's a scripture that states:

> *"Be not unequally yoked together with unbelievers for what fellowship hath righteousness with unrighteousness? And what communion hath light with darkness? And what concord hath Christ with Belial? Or what part hath he that believeth with an infidel? And what agreement hath the temple of God with idols?...." (2 Corinthians 6:14-16a)*

This should apply to many types of relationships including friendships and business partners. In reference to *"being in love without falling,"* this scripture clearly tells you not to enter into a romantic relationship with a person who is not a follower of Jesus Christ *(a Christian)* as you are. This would especially apply to a relationship with a yoke as serious and binding as marriage. Of course, this is not the only measuring rod needed when it comes to whom to marry. The person could be a true Christian, however, through your prayer life, you could receive confirmation or stop signs as to whether you should marry this person.

God has provided everything needed for you to be guided into *all* truth for your life, thus preventing costly, time-consuming errors, and *"falls."* His provisions and communication will lead you to rise and flourish into His best for you. Prayer is most important and indeed a lifeline that should never be disconnected.

Falling In Love – How To Be In Love Without Falling

✥PRAISE, WORSHIP & SERVICE✥

And Jesus answered and said unto him, Get thee behind me, Satan: for it is written, Thou shalt worship the Lord thy God, and Him only shalt thou serve.
(Matthew 4:10)

Being in love with the Lord as your first relationship priority means a life of prayer, praise, worship and service to Him. If you've truly surrendered your life to Him, your love will lead you to a desire to glorify Him and His Name in all that you do. Your desire will be to outwardly express the innate admiration, adoration, joy, thanksgiving, honor and recognition for who God is and how good He is to you. This will manifest in your music *(what you choose to listen to)*, your speech *(things you allow to come out of your mouth)* and conversations with others *(gossip, backbiting and sowing discord, for instance, may not come so easy anymore)*.

An extraordinary blessing is that He inhabits, which means He dwells, lives in the midst of your praise for Him *(Psalm 22:3)*. Where He dwells, there is much freedom and miracle-working power *(2 Corinthians 3:17)*.

To worship God means that you put no other gods before Him *(Exodus 20:3)*. It means to show profound reverence, submission and honor to Him. Unfortunately, in this day and age, there are many, many things that compete for one's worship. Most would say that they don't worship other things or people, but actions prove to the contrary. Believe it or not, some people worship jobs, money, family, love interests, sports, fame, etc. The list can go on and on. Anything or anyone who comes before God in your life is an object or individual of worship. It is called an *"idol"* or another god. I would venture to say that the concept of *"falling in love"* or the idea and anticipation of it could be identified as an idol for some. Why? Because the pursuit of it takes precedence over everything else, including God.

> *"But the hour cometh, and now is, when the true worshippers shall worship the Father in spirit and in truth: for the Father seeketh such to worship Him. God is a Spirit: and they that worship Him must worship him in spirit and in truth." (John 4:23-24)*

How to be in love without falling? Learn what it means to *"worship Him in spirit and in truth"* and live your life this way. The Lord gave me a song titled, "I Worship You With My Life." It's on my CD project of the same name. One of the main lyrics in the song says, *"Not just with lifted hands and eyes that cry, I worship You with my life."* Yes, hands go up in an act of reverence and honor towards the Lord as an act of worship. Tears flow as you tap in and experience His awesome presence and its wonderful warmth. This is well and good, but an entire life that's hidden in Him, full of daily honor, reverence, and service, He will use mightily. Your connection through prayer, praise and worship will bring revelation knowledge of how you are to serve Him with your gifts, talents and abilities. Not only will He use you to do much good, He will delight in blessing you and directing you to His very best in every area of your life. This will include a romantic love relationship more fulfilling than you ever imagined, if this is a heart's desire.

CHAPTER 11
GROWTH & DEVELOPMENT

When your love relationship with the Lord is flowing and growing, as it should, you'll have a natural desire to obey what His Word says. Even if you feel you don't have the ability to do all you read and perceive right away, you'll desire to know and do His will. You'll find a large part of His will for you written in the Bible and through your prayer communication with Him. This is how growth and development comes about. You will establish a strong foundation and increase your faith and strength to serve Him wholeheartedly. This is where church attendance comes into the picture. Many have a misconception of what church is about. It's much more than coming to a building to hear a good choir and a three-point sermon. Church is the main place where you are supposed to be taught the Word of God *(the Bible)*, how to study it, and how to live by it. Second Timothy 2:15 says, *"Study to show thyself approved unto God, a workman that needeth not to be ashamed, rightly dividing the word of truth."*

The principle of learning and studying requires the valuable input of a good teacher. The local church should be the place where you regularly receive spiritual food, biblical teaching of God's word *(Holy Bible)*, which is nourishment for you to apply to your life. It is necessary for your growth and maturity in the things of God. I like how Job put it, *"I have esteemed the words of His mouth more than my necessary food." (Job 23:12)* The Word of

Falling In Love – How To Be In Love Without Falling

God is nourishment for growth and your local church should be a major place to receive it.

You'll also learn how to apply Bible principles and teachings to your everyday life and situations. Psalm 92:13 says *"those who are planted in the house of the Lord will flourish in the courts of our God."* Therefore, being planted in a local church where the Word of God is consistently taught is where you will grow and flourish in the things of God. Your love relationship with Him will bloom into sustainable strength to handle any and everything that comes your way.

> *Let us seize and hold tightly the confession of our hope without wavering, for He who promised is reliable and trustworthy and faithful [to His Word] and let us consider [thoughtfully] how we may encourage one another to love and to do good deeds, not forsaking our meeting together [as believers for worship and instruction], as is the habit of some, but encouraging one another; and all the more [faithfully] as you see the day [of Christ's return] approaching. (Hebrews 10:23-25 AMP)*

There is a major deception in today's society that is causing people to disregard the vital importance of regularly attending a local church. I can't even tell you how many people I've talked to who say they don't go to church for one reason or another. Some say, *"I know the Man upstairs,"* but I don't go to church. Some say, *"I pray at home. That's good enough."* Some say, they do TV or online church, picking and choosing messages that feel good. Some say, they don't go to church because preachers are crooked and the church is full of hypocrites. Some say, all the church wants is your money. Yet others say, "I am The Church." This is a lie. No one person can possibly be "The Church." He can only be a part of it. These are all basic excuses that really have no merit. They are really mediocre reasons for disregarding, disrespecting, and basically dishonoring the God-ordained institution of *"The Church!"* When you become a born-again believer, you are automatically engrafted into the family of God, the Body of Christ, which is *"The Church."* The Body cannot be separated from itself. Just think about it. You can't be separated from your body. When the real you leaves your body, you are virtually dead. Similarly, when you separate yourself from the Body of Christ, *"The Church,"* you're at risk of spiritual death.

> *"Just as a body, though one, has many parts, but all its many parts form one body, so it is with Christ. For we were all baptized by one Spirit so as to form one body—whether Jews or Gentiles, slave or free—and we were all given the one Spirit to drink. Even so the Body is not made up of one part but of many." (1 Corinthians 12:12-14 NIV)*

Like it or not, you are a vital part of the Body of Christ (*The Church*). You have an important function and purpose. If you do not attend a local church, you are in disobedience and no excuse will be good enough. Especially since, when in a true love relationship with Him, He provides, protects, covers, and helps you with everything.

We all have God-given gifts, talents, and abilities that cause the Church to operate the way it should. Actually, the local church is a primary place where you can discover these things as well as your purpose in the earth and in *the Church*. In addition to your personal God-given gifts, God has provided gifts to help you achieve your full potential. The "gifts" that God provides, come in the person of *apostles, prophets, evangelists, pastors, and teachers.* He has also ordained relationships with sisters and brothers in Christ that will largely come through your local church. This is one reason we should not *"forsake the assembling of ourselves together…"* The primary person who will feed you with knowledge and understanding is your pastor, your spiritual leader. He or she is a very important person to your growth.

Falling In Love – How To Be In Love Without Falling

> *"He Himself gave some to be apostles, some prophets, some evangelists, and some pastors and teachers, for the equipping of the saints for the work of ministry, for the edifying of the body of Christ, till we all come to the unity of the faith and of the knowledge of the Son of God, to a perfect man, to the measure of the stature of the fullness of Christ; that we should no longer be children, tossed to and fro and carried about with every wind of doctrine, by the trickery of men, in the cunning craftiness of deceitful plotting, but, speaking the truth in love, may grow up in all things into Him who is the head—Christ—from whom the whole body, joined and knit together by what every joint supplies, according to the effective working by which every part does its share, causes growth of the body for the edifying of itself in love." (Ephesians 4:11-16 NKJV)*

Church is the main place where you'll be taught the Word of God. It's where you'll be trained and perfected for your new life and the work of the ministry. It's also where you'll establish new relationships with people of like faith. In a nutshell, you don't want to stop going to church, particularly as you're developing your love relationship with the Lord. It's a place of new birth, incubation, and spiritual maturity.

I know that we're in an age where most things can be done via the Internet, including church. Nonetheless, I've found that there's something powerful and peace giving that happens in the atmosphere of the sanctuary of the church that happens *no place else*, including home. When dealing with the cares of this life day after day, church is indeed a place of refuge and safety.

For some reason, many feel that people in the Church are supposed to be perfect. When someone with this mindset goes to church and encounters something less than perfection, they condemn the whole church and everyone in it. When *you* go to church, you take your issues with you. Everyone does. Some are better at hiding them than others. Church is actually a place where imperfect people go to be healed, delivered, reformed, refreshed, transformed, edified and taught how to live in an imperfect world. This means that there are bound to be issues because church is made up of people. People have issues. Just think about your own issues that you desire to be rid of. When you go to church, the issues go with you but thank God, He is not unaware of your issues. He knows everything about you *(Luke 12:7)*. He's there to meet you and helps you overcome your issues as you allow Him to.

In the Church, there *will* be some of the same stuff that goes on in the world. Along with all of the good things it represents and produces, there will be adversity, deception and much spiritual warfare. The Bible says in 1 Peter 5:8 that *"your adversary, the devil, goes to and fro seeking someone he can devour."* What better place to bring trouble than the Church with all of its Jesus followers? With adversity and deception, the goal of the adversary and his demonic forces is to prevent your spiritual growth and cause you to *fall*. Contrary to this, God uses adversity to increase spiritual growth and awareness and make you strong in the Lord and His power.

> *"In conclusion, be strong in the Lord [draw your strength from Him and be empowered through your union with Him] and in the power of His [boundless] might. Put on the full armor of God [for His precepts are like the splendid armor of a heavily-armed soldier], so that you may be able to [successfully] stand up against all the schemes and the strategies and the deceits of the devil. For our struggle is not against flesh and blood [contending only with physical opponents], but against the rulers, against the powers, against the world forces of this [present] darkness, against*

Falling In Love – How To Be In Love Without Falling

the spiritual forces of wickedness in the heavenly (supernatural) places. (Ephesians 6:10-12 AMP)

This passage in Ephesians clearly reveals that when you purpose to love the Lord and live for Him, there *will* be warfare of various degrees.

There will be people you like and those you dislike and vice versa, but you'll learn to love and respect everyone. Though people may be used and accused in the warfare *(Revelation 12:10)*, they will not be with whom you're really wrestling. I've found that demon spirits use people outside *AND* inside of the Church. Believe it or not, *demonic forces can use you* with or without your knowledge! You can also be deceived with ungodly infatuations and love interests even in the church. This is where wrong love relationships can be used in the enemy's plan to cause you to *"fall"* from God's will and purpose for your life. By the same token, your local church can be the place where you connect with a God-ordained love relationship that will cause you to rise in many ways. This is also a reason the adversary and demonic forces roam around, seeking to keep you away from your local church. *(I Peter 5:8)*.

The demonic strategy is to get people away from the very institution that will cover and increase the love, knowledge and worship of God. Offense is a huge tool used to try to separate you from God, your pastor (who feeds you with knowledge and understanding – *Jeremiah 3:15)*, and the church environment.

Whatever your warfare struggles, if handled properly, they can cause you to mature in your love relationship with the Lord. Even if you don't handle the struggle properly, it can be used to mature and bring you closer to the Lord. The warfare is a part of the transformation process *(Romans 12:2)*. Though sometimes very rough, the Lord is *all* in it! Through your love relationship with Him, you'll learn how to do warfare His way and win victory after victory.

Falling In Love – How To Be In Love Without Falling

Praise be to the LORD my Rock, who trains my hands for war, my fingers for battle. He is my loving God and my fortress, my stronghold and my deliverer, my shield, in whom I take refuge, who subdues peoples under me.
(Psalm 144:1-2 NIV)

The blessing is that as you plant yourself in the church, with your issues, God sends His word, through His Gifts, to meet you and your issues! This is where He'll teach you how to war a good warfare. No matter what your issues are, you'll learn to handle them and get free. You too can be healed, delivered, reformed, refreshed, transformed, edified and taught how to live victoriously in an imperfect world. Church is a vital part of your love relationship with the Lord and your transformation into the image of Christ *(2 Corinthians 3:18)*. This place called "Church," with all of its perks and challenges, is where you can blossom, flourish and learn how to love as God does, without *falling*.

For you who choose not to plant yourself in a local church and use the "hypocrite" excuse for your lack of church attendance, you may need to look in the mirror. *YOU* are in fact the hypocrite! The Hebrew word for "hypocrite" actually means "godless." The English definition refers to a person who pretends to have certain beliefs, attitudes or feelings when they really do not. Therefore someone pretending to know and/or love God yet doesn't go to church, is a hypocrite more so than someone who is admittedly imperfect but actually attends church regularly seeking deliverance. True hypocrites live their lives in the pretense that they can live without following the Lord's way of doing things and still be acceptable to Him. Church is an important part of His way of doing things.

❦MY INITIAL CHURCH EXPERIENCE❦

Church is the place where you will corporately worship the Lord as a part of a congregation. Personally, when the Lord came into my heart, I didn't know what to do with my newfound excitement and desire to serve. Prior to that time, life was all about me. A few days after my salvation experience, I was all about giving and doing for others! I was running around like a chicken with my head cut off locating good deeds and doing them.

> *"For we are His workmanship, created in Christ Jesus unto good works, which God hath before ordained that we should walk in them." (Ephesians 2:10)*

According to the scripture above, I was on the right track with my zeal to do good works. The only problem was that they were not the good works God had ordained for me to walk in at the time. What I was doing was actually keeping me from my time with the Lord. By the time I was done with all my good deeds and my plans to do more the next day, I was too tired to pray, read my Bible, worship or go to church. I would be so excited to get started each day, I'd convince myself that I would do my due diligence to read, pray, and worship before bedtime. Of course, before my head could hit the pillow, I was asleep. The cycle would start up again the next day.

> *"But Martha was cumbered about much serving, and came to Him, and said, Lord, dost thou not care that my sister hath left me to serve alone? Bid her therefore that she help me. And Jesus answered and said unto her, Martha, Martha, thou art careful and troubled about many things: But one thing is needful: and Mary hath chosen that good part, which shall not be taken away from her."*
> *(Luke 10:40-42)*

Falling In Love – How To Be In Love Without Falling

While in my *"good works"* mode one Wednesday, I stopped by my newfound church home. I let my late pastor know that I would not be able to attend Bible Study that night because I was busy helping others. I was so proud to tell him and just knew that I would get a pat on my back and be on my way. I was in for an awakening! Though he commended me, he very wisely ministered the truth of what was really going on. I was a baby in Christ and needed to be getting as much biblical instruction as possible in the church.

I don't remember exactly all that my late pastor said, but it boiled down to me being *"cumbered about with many things, but one thing was needful"* for me at that season of my walk with Christ. I realized that because my heart was changed and I was growing in love with the Lord, I innately wanted to do good. Although what I was doing was good, I was not necessarily doing the *"good works"* He had ordained for me at the time. I needed to be sitting at the feet of Jesus, absorbing as much of His Word as I could contain. My desire to do good was being used to distract me from getting the spiritual nourishment and knowledge I needed to grow in my love walk with the Lord.

The funny thing is that when I got to the house where I was helping out, there was a conversation going on. They didn't realize I was able to hear the conversation, which was actually about me. To make a long story short, and to spare the details, it was confirmed to me that my *"good works"* were misguided and ridiculed. It was being expressed that I was just going through one of my many phases that wouldn't last. For me, it was a painful but miraculous revelation! I had learned a valuable lesson that sent me crying out to the Lord for direction on what I was to do with my genuine desire to do good works.

I soon learned that there are so many ways the Lord can use us to serve Him and His purposes for people. All the ways He chooses to use us will truly make a difference in the lives of others. Through connecting with the church community and the pastor God leads you to, your entire life will morph or transform into fruitful, fulfilling service unto the Lord with purpose and many, many good, Godly works.

If you have the mentality that church is unnecessary, remember that Christ cannot be separated from His Body. The Body of Christ is the Church. The Church is the Body of Christ. A body separated from itself, in essence, is dead. You are an important part of a Body *(of Christ)* that is very much *alive*. You are very much needed!

In Ephesians 4, Paul talks about the Body being fitly joined together and every part being useful, every part having need of the other. In learning to be in love with the Lord, you must purpose in your heart that you will obey God's word in every area. This will include assembling yourself regularly in a local church. This is a part of the *"reasonable service"* spoken of in Romans 12:1 as you renew your mind. As you grow in love with the Lord, you won't disregard consistent church attendance *(Hebrews 10:23-25)*.

In addition to being planted in the local church that God has for you, your job is to cultivate and make sure that your heart is good ground for the Word of God to be sown into every time you attend. When His Word falls and takes root in such a heart, it produces powerful growth. There is an increase in your love for God, the things of God and people, and your life is enhanced. If you don't cultivate the soil of your heart, Satan comes immediately to steal the Word. Also, the cares of this world, deceitfulness of riches, and various types of lusts, choke the Word which then becomes unfruitful, producing nothing of substance in your life. *(Mark 4:14-20).*

Someone may be saying, *"How do I cultivate and make my heart good ground?"* Though there may be many, I believe that putting the following three principles into practice is a great start:

Falling In Love – How To Be In Love Without Falling

1. Be quick to humble yourself in love. *(John 13:34)*
2. Be quick to repent when you sin. *(1 John 1:9)*
3. Be quick to forgive others and forgive yourself. *(Matthew 6:14-15)*

　　Growing in love with God is key and a necessary precursor to any love relationship with another person.

CHAPTER 12
BE IN LOVE WITH YOU

"For You formed my innermost parts;
You knit me [together] in my mother's womb.
I will give thanks and praise to You,
for I am fearfully and wonderfully made;
Wonderful are Your works,
And my soul knows it very well.
My frame was not hidden from You,
When I was being formed in secret,
And intricately and skillfully formed [as if embroidered
with many colors] in the depths of the earth."
(Psalm 139:13-15 AMP)

Another important thing to consider in how to BE IN LOVE *WITHOUT* FALLING is your love relationship with YOU! Do you love yourself? I'm not speaking of pride and arrogance, but truly loving yourself in a healthy way, as the fearfully and wonderfully made creation God made you to be.

Are you excited about YOU and seeing God's plan and purposes unfold in your life? Do you know what His Word says about who you are? If not, you must grow in love with you, not looking to others to supply what only you can for yourself. Part of the problem with most of us, and I do say *us*, was and is what we believe about love relationships in terms of who we are individually. Many, if not most, believe that a *"fall* in love" with another individual is the key to being complete and happy. I've heard married men and women introduce their spouse as their "*better* or *other* half." Although I understand the intention, I believe the truth is, if you don't realize that you are *whole* in Christ as a single, unmarried, *(without a lover)* individual, your perspective is off point.

If you don't love yourself, you'll be very needy in a love relationship. Today, the term being used for a needy mentality is *"thirsty."* According to an April 2017 New York Times magazine article, the term *"thirsty"* is described as *"a graceless need for approval, affection or attention, one so raw that it creeps people out."* It causes you to look to the love of another to validate you. You'll even look to others to establish your worth and value. If and when they are severed from your life, you feel worthless and left without purpose. This mentality belittles the worth you already have, and will always have, based on your Creator and His creation of you. Entering into a *"love"* relationship with the wrong perspective of yourself positions you for a *"fall."*

When you don't take the time to learn, know, love and embrace who God created you to be, others can make an assessment of who they think you should be and project their purpose for you on you. A prominent minister once said, *"You can't walk in another's revelation of you, only the revelation God has given personally to you."* Lack of this personal revelation can leave you susceptible to rejection, low self-esteem, inadequacy and similar issues. It can also make you vulnerable to deception and/or victim of another's issues of inadequacy and low self-esteem. For example, say that you are confident in who you are and are *in love* with you *(in a healthy way)*. Somehow you enter a relationship with someone who doesn't have a clue who they are and never learned to love themselves. They are intimidated by your confidence in who you are. It may subconsciously produce jealousy, envy and a desire to control you and impose a self-serving purpose to you other than the one God intended. Meeting a love interest who wants to change who God created you to be, or you meeting someone and trying to mold and shape them into who you think they should be *(or think you need them to be)*, is a setup for a *fall*.

When you don't first establish and cultivate your love relationship with the Lord and yourself, it's difficult to get a real handle on your identity and purpose. The unfolding of identity and purpose is progressive revelation. This means it's slowly revealed over time. As you mature in your love relationship with the Lord, He will reveal aspects of who you are, why you're here and what you are to do with what is being revealed to you. At the same time, the enemy's demonic forces are consistently at work trying to keep revelation of who you are from you. So often, these forces will use wrong love relationships to distract, defer and deter you from this knowledge and God's purposes and plans for your life.

"For I know the plans I have for you, declares the Lord, plans to prosper you and not to harm you, plans to give you a hope and a future." (Jeremiah 29:11 NIV)

Make it your business to learn and know who you are from a spiritual, mental and emotional standpoint. Make sure that your love for you is growing and sustainable in a Godly and healthy way. You must learn what your real needs are beyond the mundane, superficial, and world-defined *"normal."* Even God doesn't focus on such things! I like what He said in I Samuel 16:7b when He sent the Prophet Samuel to find and anoint a king in the failing King Saul's place. He said, *"...For the Lord sees not as man sees; for man looks at the outward appearance, but the Lord looks at the heart."*

As you purpose to grow in love with the Lord and in love with you, He'll reveal good and bad things in and of your heart. You'll need knowledge of these things in order to be made whole, especially if you've *fallen* and have been broken in places. Some of the things He'll reveal you already know, others may be news to you. He'll also show you what to do with what is revealed. If it's good, He'll reveal how to use it for greater good. If it's bad, He'll reveal how to rid yourself of it and walk in freedom. If you pray and ask Him, He'll even help you to discern the hearts of others toward you. This is key especially when you're endeavoring to enter into covenant relationships of any kind *(romantic, platonic, business, spiritual, etc.)*. You must realize that a covenant is a spiritual agreement where both parties agree to keep their part whether the other party keeps his or her part or not. This is unlike a simple contractual agreement, which is merely a legal one where, if one party doesn't keep their part, it is broken. *(ref. NewCREEaTions.org)* These definitions are important to remember especially when it comes to a covenant relationship like marriage.

A good scripture to meditate on to solidify your wholeness in your heart is Colossians 2:9-10 included in several versions below. This will help you tremendously in building your confidence in who you are in Christ. Remember, that you are *"in Him"* and with Him, you are always enough.

> *"For in Him dwelleth all the fulness of the Godhead bodily. And ye are complete in Him, which is the head of all principality and power..."*

> *For in Christ lives all the fullness of God in a human body. So you also are complete through your union with Christ, who is the head over every ruler and authority." (NLT)*

> *"I say this because all of God lives in Christ fully, even in His life on earth. And because you belong to Christ, you are complete, having everything you need. Christ is ruler over every other power and authority." (ERV)*

Falling In Love – How To Be In Love Without Falling

You must learn what this means for you. Identity and purpose are very important. When you don't have a handle on these things, others can and will give you what they believe your identity and purpose should be based on their perception of you and their purpose and motives for you being in their life. If you're not careful, you will live much of your life based on an identity and purpose other than the one God intended for you.

When you learn and know who you are as God created you to be, you can love yourself. You can be *in love* with the unique, intelligent, intricate, intriguing, bold, strong, precious individual He so fearfully and wonderfully created for His purpose in the earth. There is no one *exactly* like you, though you may share similarities with some people. There is no one with your DNA or fingerprints. Along with many other things about you, this makes you an individual to be compared to no one. You are also not to compare yourself with anyone for any reason. Second Corinthians 10:12 reminds us, *"For we dare not make ourselves of the number, or compare ourselves with some that commend themselves."* In other words, you shouldn't try to make yourself fit into *the* mold that was made for someone else. It is much like putting a square peg into a round hole, it just won't fit.

There's absolutely nothing wrong with healthy admiration for the abilities of others, but God made you as you are and there is no comparison. God does not make junk nor does He make any mistakes *(Psalm 147:5)*. The Lord deposited a phrase in my heart years ago, *"nobody can be you better than you can."* It is so true! Learn to love and live who you are in Christ. You are His workmanship, created in Christ Jesus for His purpose, your good and the good of others *(Ephesians 2:10)*.

CHAPTER 13
YOU ARE ALWAYS ENOUGH

No matter what you've done or where you've been, who accepted or rejected you, you are enough! In many cases, you're more than enough! You can be in love with you in a healthy way because God made you in His image and likeness with a unique personality that no other person has.

> "Before I formed you in the womb I knew you; Before you were born I sanctified you; I ordained you a prophet to the nations." (Jeremiah 1:5 NKJV)

Just like Jeremiah, before you were formed in your mother's womb, God ordained you with purpose. Yours may not be as a prophet. Whatever it is, it's already established in the heart of God and waiting to be recognized and activated by you.

Mary, the mother of Jesus, had an awesome purpose and call on her life. She was highly favored and chosen by God to bring the Savior of the world into being *(Luke 1:26-38)*. She was chosen to carry, birth, nurture and raise Him for His purpose on earth. Though it was *a* great, great purpose, this was only one aspect of her life's destiny. Firstly, she was created to be a worshipper by her Father in heaven. She was also a daughter to her parents, a sister to her siblings, a wife to her husband, and a blessed mother to Jesus and several other children. Mary's life did not end when Jesus was crucified, buried and resurrected. Her other children also had their own identities and purposes to fulfill. Though theirs were different than that of Jesus in the flesh, they were significant

Falling In Love – How To Be In Love Without Falling

in the earth. They were created with purpose by God, who came to earth in the form of their earthly brother, the one and only, Savior of the world, Jesus Christ. *(John 1:1)*

Your purpose may not seem as great as someone else, but it's great in God's eyes! He appointed and established it long ago. Your job is to love God, love yourself, love others, and live to fulfill your purpose.

I've found that purpose has many aspects, assignments, facets and seasons. You may be fulfilling one aspect of your purpose in a particular season of life, and other aspects in other seasons. Whatever season you're in, your love relationship with God as well as your love for yourself and others will keep you flowing through life with direction and focus. Please remember that deception's job is to get and keep you off course of purpose, assignment and season. When you don't learn to love yourself, just the way God made you, deception has an open door to your life. When that door is open, you can live your whole life with a false identity and purpose, trying to live up to something or someone you were never meant to be. This can cause you to search endlessly for fulfillment in things outside of God and His plans and purpose for you. This can definitely lead to much confusion as well as self-hatred and ultimately, many *falls*.

This makes me think of the importance of good parenting. When babies are born, the father and mother don't usually know whom they have birthed into the earth or whom they are raising. Unless the Lord reveals some portion of the child's purpose, they just don't know. This is obvious in how many parents *(including me)* name their children with no purpose in mind. We often name them after father, mother, or other family member, some famous singer or movie star, etc. I was named after a character in a soap opera that was popular during the year of my birth. I named my son after his dad and didn't have a clue what the name meant. God knows that at 16 years old, I also didn't have a clue who I was or who my son was!

Some, who are aware of the power in a name, though they don't know the child's purpose, search out names that have profound meaning. This is a good thing. In learning to love yourself, what you call yourself matters. What's in a name? Shakespeare says, very little; however, according to the Holy Bible, there is plenty in a name!

In Genesis 17:5, God made a promise to Abram. He and his wife were far beyond childbearing age. In spite of this, God promised to make him a father of many nations and to use his wife to do it. With the promise, He changed his name to Abraham, which actually means *"father of many nations."* He changed his wife Sarai's name, to Sarah. This changed her identity from a woman who was barren with no children to *"mother of a multitude,"* which is what Sarah means. Every time anyone spoke Abraham or Sarah's names, they were speaking their new identity in line with God's promise and purpose. Similarly, Jacob, Abraham's grandson whose original name meant *"trickster,"* had an encounter with God. After the encounter, God changed his name to Israel. This changed his identity from that of a trickster to an honorable name that means, "God contends." *(Genesis 35:10).*

Proverbs 22:1 says, *"A good name is rather to be chosen than riches."* This scripture actually speaks of integrity of character and reputation more so than your actual name. Even so it is worth mentioning that your name has much to do with the forming of your character. When your name is mentioned, what type of character comes to mind? I have wondered why people nickname their babies and children names like, "Stinky," "Dumbo," "Chubby," "Killer," etc. These names follow them throughout life. Because children can be cruel and even bullies, many times these types of names cause embarrassment among their peers and can cause serious rejection and esteem issues.

Falling In Love – How To Be In Love Without Falling

Parenting in and of itself is an awesome call and purpose! Parents, too, are created, born and raised. It's a perpetual cycle of parents being created, producing and raising more parents. Parents must be fully cognizant of the fact that they are not raising a clone of themselves or what they may have aspired to be. It's important to love and observe the child and train them up in the admonition of the Lord *(Proverbs 22:6; Ephesians 6:4)*. It's also important to point them as arrows in the direction of their true identity, gifting, talents and honorable desires *(Psalm 127:4)*. I wonder if any of the U.S. Presidents' parents knew they were raising great leaders?

Returning focus to the concept of *"being in love with you,"* you may need to stop and take a look at your own upbringing, background and love relationship history. What type of parental examples did you have growing up? What was modeled before you as a child? Did it set the stage for your concept of what a love relationship should look like? If you felt starved for love as a child, you may spend much of your life looking for it, often in all of the wrong places. Many people carry unresolved childhood issues into adult relationships, thinking that some love interest has the answer to the issue.

Personally, I was always looking for love and attention that I never seemed to be able to get enough of as a child. It was not that love from my family was not there, it just never seemed to be enough or the type of love I *thought* I needed. Consequently, I ventured out to find love enough to fill the void I always felt. Needless to say, my search resulted in several *"falls"* until I encountered the Lord and gave Him my life. It wouldn't have been so bad, except children were brought into the picture in the course of my *"falls."* Of course, my children suffered because of my selfish, unrelenting search for love! They were actually innocent, unsuspecting bystanders who didn't understand why they couldn't get the love they needed. God knows I had no business becoming

Falling In Love – How To Be In Love Without Falling

a parent in the emotional state I was in for so long. Immature children who don't know who they are should not become parents.

According to Ecclesiastes 1:9, there is nothing new under the sun. I've noticed that many young ladies are still being deceived as they search for love, identity and purpose. Many often prematurely and illegitimately become parents of several children with multiple fathers before locating the proper love of self. Some inadvertently try to trap young men they *"fall"* in love with, as they believe that sexual sin leading to pregnancy and having a child will secure the relationship. Still searching for love, they may birth several children by different young men. Often, because the men feel trapped, the relationship *"fails"* leaving the young lady alone and the children without the love, guidance and provision of two, loving parents. Having child after child, the young ladies don't realize that all of their energy is going to be swallowed up in motherhood, not romantic love. This often leads to extremely bad parenting, neglect and abuse of the children. On the other hand, such circumstances can make for extremely good mothers and fathers who work tirelessly to make sure their children receive the love and nurturing they need despite the failure of their relationships.

The point here is that lack of love for self can lead to fall after fall for everyone involved. The good news is that God knows and loves us even before we learn to love Him or ourselves *(Romans 5:8)*! There is forgiveness and restoration into vibrant and purposeful life regardless of the circumstance. Forgiveness and restoration is what the Lord is all about, particularly when one recognizes, repents and submits to His will and way of doing things.

CHAPTER 14
ILLEGITIMATE BUT ORDAINED

I will never forget a statement that was dropped into my spirit years ago based on the story of Hagar and Ishmael in Genesis 16. God had promised Abram *(re-named Abraham)* a son. His wife *(Sarai, renamed Sarah)*, who couldn't conceive a child, had a bright idea. She instructed her husband to sleep with her young handmaid (Hagar) in order to bring God's promise of a child to pass *(Genesis 16:2)*. Well, a child was born out of the situation. I call this an illegitimate child because he wasn't the child God had promised. The statement that was dropped into my spirit was *"illegitimate but ordained."* Even though Ishmael, whose name meant, *"God will hear,"* was illegitimate; he was an authorized and ordained human being. Not only that, he was the legitimate seed of Abraham, though not the promised seed. In spite of how he got here, he had a life to live with purpose just like everyone else who is born. He, too, needed love, nurturing and guidance as he walked through life. Just like every other person, he had no choice in how he came into the earth. Yet, because of the circumstances surrounding his conception and birth, his road to purpose was a rocky one.

God had promised a child to Abraham and Sarah. Although what Sarah did in giving the woman over to her husband was acceptable as a custom in that era, it was not God's best. Therefore, Sarah, Abraham consenting, took it upon herself to bring an illegitimate party into the picture, Hagar, which produced a legitimate child in that he was the seed of Abraham, but *"illegitimate"* in that the child's mother was not Sarah.

Well, as God would have it, some time later, the promised, *"legitimate"* child *(Isaac)* was born *(Genesis 21:2-30)*. He grew along with the illegitimate child who was his half-brother. When friction occurred between the two mothers about the children, one of them had to go! Of course, it was the illegitimate one *(Genesis 21:10-11)*. Hagar and Ishmael were sent away from home with nothing but a loaf of bread and some water. They were sent into a place of wilderness to fend for themselves. This child was uprooted from his true father and the only home he knew. He had to watch the hardship his mom endured and the struggle of surviving in the wilderness. He was the product of a broken home from the very beginning. Even though this happened, the child and his mom were still loved by God and had purpose to fulfill *(Genesis 21:12-13; 17-18)*.

Hagar was really a single mom in that she was simply Abraham's concubine and his wife's handmaid. She was a slave; however, she did have a home there where Ishmael had the love and guidance of his father. At the same time, Hagar was in a subordinate situation because she was not *the* true wife of her son's father. There was always tension between Sarai and Hagar until finally one particular situation was the last straw in Sarai's heart. She told her husband to send Hagar and Ishmael away *(Genesis 21:8-10)*. Abram was bothered by it and didn't want to do it. However, God told him to send them away *(Genesis 21:11-13)*. Not only had God spoken to Hagar about who Ishmael was to be *(Genesis 16:11-12)*, He also told Abram that He would bless Ishmael and make a nation from him because he was legitimately Abraham's seed *(Genesis 21:13)*.

Hagar, whose identity and worth was steeped in slavery and bondage, was now in a different place. She was no longer a slave and now needed to learn and love herself and walk in the identity of a free woman. As a slave, her identity and purpose was hidden within that of those who owned, supported and controlled her life. Ishmael went from being the son of a powerful man of God to a homeless teenager scrambling in the wilderness with his mom. What a horrible, shocking rejection that ultimately resulted in freedom and a huge initial step into God's promise of becoming a blessed nation of people!

So, Hagar and Ishmael went through an abrupt, life-altering experience. They were suddenly homeless for a time, having no idea what they would encounter being sent out into a desert place. Did their lives end because of this? No! Even though at one point when their water was depleted, it appeared that they were going to die, God did not allow it. In fact, He lovingly intervened, guided them to a well of water, and gave them a word of inspiration that launched them into the new life He desired for them. God was with them and it turned out that the desert place they were cast into became their place of refuge. The wilderness became their home and where Ishmael grew into not only a mighty archer, but also the mighty nation God promised. *(Genesis 21:15-20)*

Can you relate to Hagar and Ishmael's situation in some way? Can you imagine the struggle with rejection, condemnation, unforgiveness, bitterness and similar emotions they both had to overcome? There *is* nothing new under the sun. Many of us were illegitimately born and raised by single parents, yet ordained of God with identity and purpose just like those who were raised in a two-parent home. Many have been betrayed in crazy relationship situations similar to Hagar's, where your self-esteem and worth were challenged. More than likely, you came out of it questioning if anyone could love you, including you. No matter what your birthright, upbringing or relationship history, loving God, living your life in a God-ordained manner, and being in love with you will help to bring you through any wilderness experience and to a place of rest. Eventually, you'll realize that being in love with the you God created will help you to set and keep standards that will help you avoid unnecessary *"falls"* into situations of bondage.

❦SELF-EVALUATION❦

Now would be a good time to evaluate where you are as a young lady or young man. Locate yourself and the love you have for yourself. Do you love yourself enough to follow God's way of doing things? Why? Because it's the very best way!

"As for God, His way is blameless.
The word of the LORD is tested [it is perfect, it is faultless];
He is a shield to all who take refuge in Him.
For who is God, but the LORD?
Or who is a rock, except our God,
The God who encircles me with strength
And makes my way blameless?"
(Psalm 18:30-32 AMP)

Loving yourself is an important key to avoiding falls. When you have healthy self-esteem, and you know who you are in Christ, it's difficult to be deceived. You're not so needy that you'll accept whoever comes your way with a polished, or not so polished, exterior and a charismatic persona. Don't be needy! When you're needy, your view will be distorted and you won't recognize obvious stop signs.

Once, my first-born son and I stopped at a fast food restaurant. My son is tall and handsome and has a beautiful smile. When we approached the young lady at the counter, he greeted her with, *"Hey pretty girl."* It amazed me how *immediately* she smiled from ear to ear and blushed openly. It was as if everything and everyone else at the counter disappeared and she was swallowed up in that smile and compliment. I actually had to wave my hand in front of her face to get her attention to take our order as she stared at him. It was obvious that those were words she didn't hear often. He won her over with that compliment and a certain amount of natural charisma. She was obviously distracted. My point is that she seemed vulnerable, needy, and easily flattered to the point of distraction, which made her a good candidate for a *"fall."*

Paul said in Philippians 4:19, *"But my God shall supply all your NEED according to His riches in glory by Christ Jesus."* That applies to all born-again believers. There is no need to be needy when He is the supplier of everything.

"Be anxious for nothing, but in everything by prayer and supplication, make your request known unto God, and the peace of God, which passes all understanding shall guard your heart and mind in Christ Jesus."
(Philippians 4:6-7)

As you patiently evaluate the degree of your love for you, realize that no matter who your parents were and how you were raised, if you're born again, God is your Father and His way is perfect. God created you in His image. You exist for purpose because He created you with purpose. Because of who He is, you can love yourself without reservation with all of your issues and oddities. When you're obedient, He's your Father. When you're disobedient and mess up, He's still your Father. No matter what, He's your Father. He will always be there for you. I like what David said in Psalm 139:7-8, *"Whither shall I go from thy spirit? Or wither shall I flee from thy presence? If I ascend up into heaven, thou art there: if I make my bed in hell, behold, thou art there."* If for no other reason, and there are many others, you can love yourself!

Love, embrace and be content with the *"you"* that God created. As you grow in the knowledge of Him and His will for you, you'll desire what and whom He desires for you. Psalm 37:4 talks about delighting yourself in the Lord and *Him* giving you the desires of your heart. Amazingly, as you truly delight your*self* in Him, your desires actually begin to change and line up with His desires for you. As this takes place, you can avoid the proverbial *"fall"* and *"rise"* into His very best for you. As you follow your Father's lead in obedience, He will show you how to *"be in love without falling.*

CHAPTER 15
LEARN TO LOVE ALL PEOPLE

While completing this book, the world is in the midst of the Coronavirus pandemic. Many people have died from it. In addition, there is much racial and political tension in the United States due to the highly publicized deaths of some Black individuals at the hands of police officers as well as other citizens. Many believe we are very close to the "End Times," the return of Jesus Christ and the "catching away" of the Church *(1 Thessalonians 4:17)*. There is protesting and looting in addition to rising occurrences of gun violence resulting in more crime and death. This includes Black on Black, White on White, Hispanic on Hispanic, and etc. crime within the respective communities. Fear, hatred and bitterness are having a real impact throughout the world. Much of the world's population is hurting and going through the most trying times of their lives. Frankly, the need for the power and glory that comes through real *(God's)* love has overwhelmingly increased with all of this evil. In addition to salvation through Jesus Christ and seeking Him like never before, learning to genuinely love and forgive all people is key.

The last, but not least, thing I'd like you to consider in how to *BE IN LOVE WITHOUT FALLING* is your love for all who were created in the image of God *(Genesis 1:27)*, people in general. Because God is Love, He commands and expects us to love all people *(Romans 13:8)*. When you love God and yourself in a healthy way, you *can* love others in a healthy way as well. Often, if you have a problem loving yourself, you may also have a problem loving other people and receiving love. This may have a significant effect on a potential romantic love interest.

To be clear, you don't have to *"be in love"* with everyone. You don't even have to like everyone, but to sincerely love and respect mankind in general is huge! There are many places in the Bible where there are instructions to love others. Matthew 22:39 says to *"love your neighbors as you love yourself."* John 13:34 says to *"love one another as God has loved you."* The Lord doesn't stop there! Matthew 5:43-44 says to even *"love your enemies"* and to actually *"pray for those who hate you and despitefully use and persecute you."* Although this is difficult, it's not impossible. Why? Because *"with God, all things are possible" (Matthew 19:26)* and there is *"nothing too difficult for Him" (Genesis 18:14)*, including eliminating your disdain and disrespect for other people groups. I realize more and more how serious God is about us loving all people as He does. As we grow in love with Him, it's impossible to avoid the *"love one another"* command.

Someone may say, "What's this got to do with being in love without falling in a romantic relationship?" I say, EVERYTHING! Human beings, though created by God Almighty who is perfect, are flawed. David put it like this in *Psalm 51:5,"...born in sin, shaped in iniquity."* Romans 3:23 begins with, *"For all have sinned....,"* even so, before we enter the womb, we are created in the image of God. We are then born into the earth with unique personalities, gifts, and abilities. We also have individual idiosyncrasies, behaviors and challenges.

From the point of conception on to birth and after, the process of maturation and transformation continues throughout all stages of life. Everyone develops preferences, likes, dislikes, and prejudices, not to mention all of the experiences that shape who we ultimately become. It's natural to personally prefer a particular

Falling In Love – How To Be In Love Without Falling

type of person over another. This is exactly why it takes conscious effort to love others as God loves us all.

As you learn to love all people, you will be more open to connect with a love interest that may not necessarily be an obvious preference that you're aware of. Just say that your preference is really based on some superficial attributes in one's appearance. As we mature, we develop perspectives and our own way of thinking and doing things that coincide with our likes and dislikes. These likes and dislikes include the types of people we'll choose to love or not. You know what I mean, tall, dark and handsome vs. short, pale, and not so handsome, Black vs. White, Chinese vs. Hispanic, Republican vs. Democrat, you name it. Some of the best love relationships I know are people who would not have necessarily chosen each other. They connected beyond the superficial preference and built an enduring love that is without condition.

Believe it or not some people have the nerve to brand other people as *"unlovable."* The word may bring a picture of certain people to mind. This is actually an immature mentality that, if taken too far, causes separation and love loss. Until we properly mature, we feel that our way is always the way to go. Anyone who doesn't agree and conform to our way of being or doing things may be deemed as unlovable, at least for a time. Truth is, you may be considered *"unlovable"* to somebody. Bottom line is, there is no such person in God's eyes and He wants us to have the same mentality. Everyone is deserving of love because of who God is and the fact that He made every individual to receive love. This makes every individual lovable.

This brings me to my main objective in this chapter. It's a normal, human propensity to want others to see things from our own perspective. When we are dealing with others, this tendency causes our differences to surface and may cause conflict, which God is very much aware of. Thus, in His infinite wisdom, it was necessary for Him to instruct us to do things like, love one another *(John 13:34)*, forgive one another *(Colossians 3:13)*, be at peace with all men *(Romans 12:18)*, etc. It's all a part of the process of being transformed into the true image of Christ *(Colossians 3:10)*. If these points are not enough, there is 1 Corinthians 13:

> *"Though I speak with the tongues of men and of angels, but have not love, I have become sounding brass or a clanging cymbal. And though I have the gift of prophecy, and understand all mysteries and all knowledge, and though I have all faith, so that I could remove mountains, but have not love, I am nothing. And though I bestow all my goods to feed the poor, and though I give my body to be burned, but have not love, it profits me nothing. Love suffers long and is kind; love does not envy; love does not parade itself, is not puffed up; does not behave rudely, does not seek its own, is not provoked, thinks no evil; does not rejoice in iniquity, but rejoices in the truth; bears all things, believes all things, hopes all things, endures all things. Love never fails."*
> *(1 Corinthians 13:1-8 NKJV)*

The fact that God gives us the ability to love everyone is evident in little children. Before they are taught otherwise, they are great examples of how the Lord would have us to love each other. They don't care who you are, what your ethnicity is or the color of your skin. If you put children in a room together, they just gravitate to each other in a loving way. For example, while visiting at a hospital, I observed two three-year-olds near a play area. They had never met, nor had their parents. They ran to each other, embraced and even kissed each other on the mouth! It was a big surprise to all of the adults that were around, but seemed totally natural for them. It was sheer, uninhibited love in action and I'll never forget it! They had never met and knew absolutely nothing about each other, and it didn't matter. Children have to be taught

Falling In Love – How To Be In Love Without Falling

caution and wisdom. Sad to say, but they also have to be *taught* discrimination, prejudice, hatred and racism. Until then, they are full of uninhibited, unbridled, unconditional and unfailing love.

As we mature, there are all types of good and bad growth lessons. We make mistakes, commit trespasses against others and experience trials, and tribulations. The blessing is that all life experiences, good, bad and indifferent, count for something. Until we accept Jesus as Savior, sin has dominion over us. Like it or not, we act out sinful ways which often hurt others as well as ourselves. Learning to love others, separating them from their sinful acts, is a major part of life's lessons that many never continue after a certain age or experience. Let's look at the example of some abused children. In spite of what they endure, they love their abusive parents unconditionally and may quickly forgive over and over again. They often tell no one of the abuse. This is because they were created by Love and for love. They keep the hope that the abuse will one day stop. The abuse they experience is a perversion of the enemy producing fear and much confusion. Love is powerful even in the midst of fear and confusion! However, love and the effects of abuse in it is a whole nother story for another time!

The way you live out your love walk in basic non-romantic relationships has everything to do with being in love and staying in a romantic relationship without *"falling."*

As we go throughout life, we must understand that everyone has flaws. We're all in the same type of skin, so to speak, and we all bleed the same color blood. It is so important to realize this especially when it comes to romantic *"love"* relationships. When you meet someone that you're attracted to or become infatuated with, for a while, they seem flawless. At least you'd like to think they are. You choose to ignore negative things about them or explain them away to a degree. Why? It's because you desire to see *only* the best in them. As time passes and you become

Falling In Love – How To Be In Love Without Falling

familiar with one another, infractions that can't be ignored begin piling up. The flaws, which have been there all along, may now seem intolerable or even offensive. Couple this with your own flaws, which we all often ignore or deny, and the result is opposition and challenges to the concept of unconditional love and forgiveness.

Loving others in general is good training for "being in love *without falling*." As you enter close relationships, flaws surface along with more opportunities to learn how to love with or without condition. Hopefully, your goal is that of love without condition.

Many times, we try to "correct" the flaws, when, in fact, they may simply be a part of the individual's personality. This is where many love relationships *"fall."* You see the flaw, get the idea in the back of your mind, "Oh, I can change that;" when in fact, it's a part of the person that can't be altered. Frankly, you may find that since you can't change it, you can't tolerate it. This happens often in marriage and is the basis for many divorces. It's actually how a person could be so much "in love" in the beginning of a relationship and actually be willing to kill that same person in the end!

As we encounter and live with people in our everyday lives, we must learn to love without condition, as God does. This includes family, friends, neighbors, co-workers, church members, strangers, etc. This means no matter what people do or don't do, say or don't say, we must find a way to love them anyway. Some of you may have to love from a distance based on circumstances, but still love them. This is a difficult thing, especially when there is so much division, opposition, prejudice, racism, discriminatory tension and resistance to real love and unity in the world we live in. Please remember that disagreement and hatred are not synonymous!

CHAPTER 16
LEARN TO FORGIVE ALL PEOPLE

There's a prayer in the Bible that is generally known as "The Lord's Prayer" *(Matthew 6:9-13)*. It occurred to me one day that, quite miraculously, most people all over the world somehow have been taught this prayer to some degree. Many know it well. This is amazing to me! Even people who profess to be atheist or agnostic may actually know this prayer. Whenever anyone begins to recite, *"Our Father, which art in heaven, etc..."* people readily chime in. When asked, some can but many can't recall when or how they learned it. This is the prayer that Pope Frances asked Christians all over the world to recite amid the Coronavirus pandemic. The only other passage of scripture that I believe is known nearly as well is Psalm 23 which begins, *"The Lord is my Shepherd I shall not want..."* etc. In my opinion, this shows the love of God for all mankind in providing a perfect prayer that many have been taught, have memorized and prayed at some time or other.

Once during one of the difficult times in my life, I was searching for a prayer that had been written by my pastor. It is an excellent prayer, packed with biblical declarations and scriptures that cover many areas that I need to pray about regularly. For some odd reason, I couldn't locate that particular prayer when it was usually easily accessible in my office. While searching for it, I heard in my spirit, "Why don't you pray *My* prayer?" I immediately knew exactly which prayer it was.

Falling In Love – How To Be In Love Without Falling

Although I could recite the prayer, I knew I was supposed to actually locate it in the Bible and study it as I prayed. I grabbed my Bible and looked up where I would find it. As I began to read and pray through Matthew 6:9-13, I received revelation after revelation that I had never noticed before. I had read this passage many times, often skimming over it, taking for granted that I already knew it. I, too, had learned this prayer long before I gave my life to Jesus. However, it was obvious that I didn't really *know* it at all, at least, not the way the Lord revealed it to me that day.

It included everything necessary to pray through my immediate situation and actually applied to life in general. It encompassed worship, submitting to His Kingdom and His will in Heaven and earth, daily provisions, forgiveness of sins, and deliverance from evil. When I really dissected it, I realized that this prayer generally covered every area of basic life! *"Amen"* at the end of the prayer means, *"so be it,"* and the prayer is done. However, this particular time, I was prompted to read beyond the end of the prayer. In light of what I was praying about, what I read in the following verses stirred my heart.

> *"For if ye forgive men their trespasses, your heavenly Father will also forgive you: But if ye forgive not men their trespasses, neither will your Father forgive your trespasses." (Matthew 6:14-15)*

In this entire passage of scripture, the concept of *"forgiveness"* is mentioned three times, specifically verses 12, 14 and 15. Although I don't recall everything I was praying about that day, I know that those verses brought deliverance from a situation that was trying to plant unforgiveness and bitterness in my heart. I tell you; those last two verses practically jumped off the page at me and is a principle that I have strived even harder to live by ever since!

Falling In Love – How To Be In Love Without Falling

I chose to share my experience because prayer and forgiveness are major factors in being in love without falling. This is definitely a lifelong learning process as people come in and out of your life. Not only are you commanded by Jesus to love your neighbor, you are told to love your enemies as well as yourself. Unfortunately, there are times when your neighbor and your enemy can be one and the same. There are also times when you can be enemy to yourself. In any case, the basic concept of the command is not easy. Personally, I don't see how it can truly be done without faith and a flourishing love relationship with God!

When we love the Lord, as we should, we want to be obedient to His Word. Forgiveness, loving enemies and praying for them is difficult, if not impossible, without the help of the Lord, real faith and knowledge of and agreement with biblical principles.

Forgiveness is a huge part of loving others without condition. This is mainly because we are all flawed and we commit infractions against each other whether in word, thought or deed. That's what forgiveness is all about. If there's no infraction, there's no need to forgive. If you don't learn the principle of loving others without condition and quick forgiveness, you won't be able to remain in a fruitful love relationship. A fall is inevitable without it! You can count on being disappointed and hurt to some degree in any relationship that's worth its salt. If you practice loving all people, your heart will be prepared to manage and thrive in a *"til death do you part"* relationship. Being in love without falling requires unconditional love and very, very frequent forgiveness.

Many people carry things like unforgiveness, bitterness and hatred in their hearts. If you were like I was before accepting Christ, you didn't know how to release those who hurt you. You just stuffed the hurt and pain and held on to every little infraction. At the drop of a hat, no matter how long ago the offense was committed, you could pull your hurts out of that emotional hat of unforgiveness and use it to create a pity party often resulting in a fight. If the present person in your life does anything even slightly resembling something that once hurt you, there was *"hell"* to pay, so-to-speak.

Stockpiled unforgiveness, bitterness and hatred produce a type of pandemic that infects the heart of the person carrying it. These things can clog up the heart's flow to experiencing a trusting, loving relationship that can endure. It will also have a negative effect on those around you.

> *"Follow peace with all men, and holiness, without which no man shall see the Lord: Looking diligently lest any man fail of the grace of God; lest any root of bitterness springing up trouble you, and thereby many be defiled;"*
> *(Hebrews 12:14-16)*

So, if you want to be in love without falling, you'll need to learn to truly forgive and release those who may have hurt, harmed, or abused you. Please know that learning this will not necessarily be easy but it will be so worth it! Believe it or not, you can totally do it and it would be so good if you truly learned to practice this before you meet the person with whom you intend to spend the rest of your natural life with.

> *"Above all, have fervent and unfailing love for one another, because love covers a multitude of sins [it overlooks unkindness and unselfishly seeks the best for others]."*
> *(1 Peter 4:8 AMP)*

The love that covers a multitude of sins includes your sins as well as the sins of others. God's love covers your multitude of sins and gives you the ability to cover and forgive the multitude of others' sins.

❧FORGIVENESS PRAYER/DELIVERANCE❧

Father, I repent of holding unforgiveness, bitterness and offense in my heart. I ask you to forgive me and cleanse me from all unrighteousness. I now forgive and release any and everyone who has hurt or trespassed against me. Lord, I forgive myself and I forgive (name the people who come to mind) and I release them from my heart right now in the Name of Jesus. Father, by faith and with Your help I choose to forget all that was done and I thank you for helping me to cast down any thoughts about it that may crop up in the future. I ask You to help me to love ALL people, as You would have me to love them, and be quick to resist and forgive any offense that comes my way. I renounce and command every spirit of racism, hatred, bigotry, discrimination, bitterness, unforgiveness, offense and any associated spirits to GO NOW, in Jesus' Name! I repent of sinful attitudes and thoughts that cause unforgiveness! I believe I receive Your freedom, ability and wisdom to walk in love and forgiveness with anyone, in any situation! I pray all of these things in Jesus' Name, Amen!

Praying this prayer in sincerity has put something powerful into motion for you! True repentance is a powerful tool of transformation and a huge step forward in your *love* walk. I must remind you not to be ignorant of Satan's devices *(2 Corinthians 2:11)*. Just as Jesus was tempted when He was led into the wilderness *(Matthew 4:1-11)*, you too will be tempted with opportunities to receive offense and hold unforgiveness. Guess what? You have the ability to resist the temptation and to walk in true love and forgiveness! Not only can you walk in victory over unforgiveness, you have the ability to truly love and forgive over and over and over again no matter what the infraction. Take a look

Falling In Love – How To Be In Love Without Falling

at *Matthew 18:21-22 (AMP), '...Lord, how many times will my brother sin against me and I forgive him and let it go, up to seven times?' Jesus answered him, "I say to you, not up to seven times, but seventy times seven."* The principle here is to forgive as many times as necessary. This is so useful if applied in all relationships but especially in close romantic relationships between flawed human beings, which we all are. It definitely requires great patience and strength!

> *"But those who wait upon the Lord [who expect, look for, and hope in Him] Will gain new strength and renew their power; They will lift up their wings [and rise up close to God] like eagles [rising toward the sun]; They will run and not become weary, They will walk and not grow tired."*
> *(Isaiah 40:31 AMP)*

As a flawed individual, perfecting your relationship with God, yourself and others will require waiting on the Lord, serving Him wholeheartedly. As you serve Him you will not only grow in the knowledge of Him, but the practice of forgiveness will become easier and easier. Your strength will be consistently renewed. You will be able to freely walk and wait without yielding to weariness, for whatever, wherever and whomever He has in store for your future!

Today, consider yourself void of the conflicting confession and threat of the proverbial *"fall in love"* because now you know *"how to be in love without falling!"*

> *"Now unto Him that is able to keep you from falling, and to present you faultless before the presence of His glory with exceeding joy. Amen." (Jude 24)*

ABOUT THE AUTHOR

Vanessa Dale Coleman is a committed follower of Jesus Christ. She is the wife of Chester Coleman and together they have four grown children, six grandchildren, and four great grandchildren. She heads Songs for Life Ministries, which is dedicated to producing anointed Bible-based songs, books, and blogs along with creative literature and images.

Her testimony and God-given gifts and abilities are first hand proof of what the power of God, through Jesus Christ, can do for a seemingly incorrigible individual. The Lord has brought her through rejection and poverty as a child, teenage pregnancy, major confusion, a life of crime, drug, alcohol and nicotine addiction, an abusive marriage along with other ungodly relationships, and more. She is now a licensed/ordained Minister/Teacher of the Gospel, a worship leader, songwriter, recording artist, author, and certified graphic designer. She ministers the Word of God, without compromise, in unique and diverse manners. Her heart's desire is to see all types of people delivered from hateful demonic bondages that so often develop due to a lack of love and clear understanding of it!

SUGGESTED READING

"Now What, A Guide for New Christians"
by Ralph W. Harris – ISBN 0-88243-558-2

"Why Tongues"
By Kenneth E. Hagin ISBN 0-89276-051-6

"Prevailing Prayer"
by Pastor Teresa Thiongo' - Kitale, Kenya

"Prayers That Avail Much"
(Commemorative Gift Edition)
by Germaine Copeland / Word Ministries, Inc.

"Loves Me, Love Me Not – Help For The Hurting"
by Pastor Pricellious J. Burruss – ISBN 0-9667410-3-X

"Hindrances To Receiving Your Mate"
by Bishop Richard Burruss – ISBN 0-9667410-2-1X

"To All My Baby Mamas –
Single Parenting Without Bitterness"
by Cortaiga S. Collins – ISBN 978-1-4984-9287-4

"Fear Exposed"
by Kacie Starr Long - ISBN 979-8-65645-0911

"Making Your Marriage and Life Marvelous"
by Bishop E.L. Warren - ISBN 1-56043-228-4

"Hinds Feet on High Places"
by Hanna Hurnard – ISBN 0-8423-1429-6

"My Utmost For His Highest" Daily Devotional
by Oswald Chambers – ISBN 1-57748-142-9

Songs For Life Products

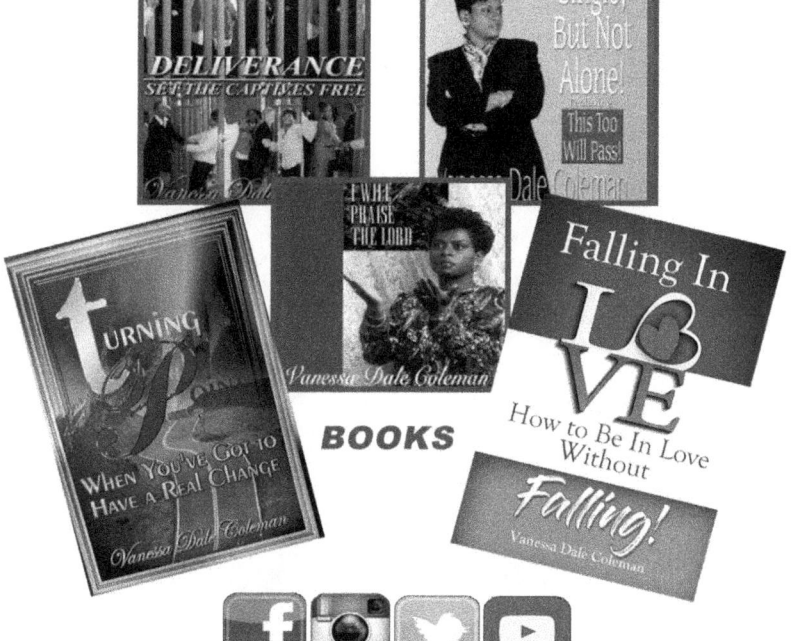

Vanessa Dale Coleman
Songs For Life Ministries

VanessaDaleColeman.com
SongsFL1@sbcglobal.net or Vanessa4807@gmail.com
PO Box 23360 - St. Louis, MO 63156
314.616.7176

www.ingramcontent.com/pod-product-compliance
Lightning Source LLC
Chambersburg PA
CBHW071124090426
42736CB00012B/2001